Deliciously Irish

FOR LOUIS, EVA
AND CHRISTINE

Deliciously Irish

THE BEST OF IRISH COUNTRY COOKING

NUALA CULLEN

FOOD PHOTOGRAPHY BY TONY BRISCOE
LANDSCAPE PHOTOGRAPHY BY MICHAEL DIGGIN

PAVILION

CONTENTS

Left: Bluebells bloom in spring at Killarney National Park in County Kerry.

INTRODUCTION

The vision of ancient Celtic Ireland that has come down to us through folklore and poetry is of a land of plenty, where poetry and music were among the important occupations of the people, and honour and hospitality went hand in hand.

Through the centuries, hospitality continued to be a matter of honour, for rich and poor alike. Nearer to our own times, in the eighteenth and nineteenth centuries, successive travellers to Ireland invariably commented on the lavish welcome, the rich variety and quantity of food and the large numbers of persons entertained. The ill-fated dependence upon the potato by almost one-quarter of the population, however, and the tragic aftermath of the failure of the potato crop in the successive famines of the 1840s, is all too well known. Life changed profoundly for many people as a consequence, and the tradition of prodigal hospitality was almost swept away.

Ireland, however, is a natural food-producing country and, in recent decades, extensive research has produced an improved understanding of the best production methods for our food resources, creating a true land of plenty. Irish products are now in demand all over Europe. There has been a renaissance in Irish cooking, too: a new generation of Irish chefs, cosmopolitan in their training but with roots in their own tradition, are creating a discernibly Irish style of professional cooking, which allows the excellent raw materials to speak for themselves. We are also fortunate in Ireland that many of the festival days are still observed, even if only in perfunctory way. Such feast days obviously put the emphasis on seasonal ingredients, and the recipes included in this book aim to give an idea of some of the dishes that have been in common use in Ireland for many hundreds of years (with a few exceptions).

I hope that you will enjoy them and that they will contribute in some measure to the enjoyment of your guests and the conviviality of the dinner table, a pleasure as important in Ireland today as it has been for centuries.

Right: The rolling hills of County Kerry.

STARTERS

MUSSELS WITH BACON AND RED WINE

SERVES 6 AS A STARTER OR 4 AS A MAIN COURSE

'Lord Smart (to Neverout): Tom, they say fish should swim thrice.

Neverout: How is that, my Lord?

Lord Smart: Why, Tom, first it should swim in the Sea (Do you mind me?), then it should swim in Butter; and at last Sirrah, it should swim in good Claret.'

Jonathan Swift, Polite Conversation

2 litres/3½ pints live mussels
240 ml/8 fl oz red wine
2 tablespoons butter
1 fresh thyme sprig
6 streaky bacon rashers, chopped
4 shallots
2 garlic cloves, finely chopped
3 large ripe tomatoes, de-seeded and chopped
1 tablespoon plain flour
2 tablespoons chopped fresh flat-leaved parsley, plus extra to garnish
salt and freshly ground black pepper
fresh crusty bread, to serve

Clean the mussels thoroughly, discarding any that are broken or which don't close when sharply tapped, and put them in a large saucepan, with the wine. Cover, bring to the boil and cook for 2 minutes, shaking the pan from time to time, until the mussels are open. Remove the mussels to a bowl, discarding any that do not open. Strain the liquid carefully into a bowl, discarding any sand or grit.

Melt 1 tablespoon butter in a saucepan, add the thyme and bacon and cook until crisp. Then add the shallots and garlic and cook until soft. Add the tomatoes.

Blend the remaining butter and the flour together and stir into the saucepan, a piece at a time, stirring until the flour is cooked and the sauce is smooth. Add the mussel liquid gradually, stirring until the sauce has thickened. If it is too thick, add a little water. Reheat the mussels in the sauce for a few moments, then stir in the parsley. Check and adjust the seasoning. Garnish with parsley and serve with fresh crusty bread.

Previous Page: Fishing boats at Dingle Peninsula in Lough Gill, County Kerry.

SOUSED HERRINGS

SERVES 4–6

The herring was once a staple of the Irish diet, and its seasonal reappearance was greeted with pleasure by rich and poor alike. Sousing, a simple way of preserving fish, became very popular in its own right. The sousing liquid here is a mild one, so if you like your herrings hot, leave them in the cold marinade for a few hours before cooking to develop the flavours.

8–10 herring fillets
8–10 shallots
2–3 bay leaves
1 onion, finely sliced
1 tablespoon chopped fresh parsley
small boiled potatoes, to serve

FOR THE MARINADE

300 ml/½ pint cider or white wine vinegar
300 ml/½ pint dry cider or white wine
2 teaspoons juniper berries, slightly crushed
½ tsp chilli powder or chopped fresh chillies, or to taste
1–2 tablespoons each of brown sugar, mustard seeds and black peppercorns

Boil the marinade ingredients together gently for a few minutes. Cool and allow to infuse for 30 minutes.

Preheat the oven to 150°C/300°F/Gas Mark 2. Lay out the fish fillets on a board and arrange a peeled shallot and a bay leaf on each half. Roll up and secure with a cocktail stick. Arrange in an ovenproof dish, scatter the onion slices over the top and pour the marinade into the dish. Cover with foil and bake for 30–40 minutes.

Garnish with the parsley and serve with small boiled potatoes. To serve cold, cool before packing into a plastic box, which will allow the cooking liquid to cover them, and chill, overnight if possible. Serve with pickled onions or gherkins with mustard or horseradish sauce on the side. They will keep for 2–3 days in the fridge.

COD'S ROE & COD'S ROE PÂTÉ

SERVES 4 AS A STARTER OR 2 AS A LUNCH DISH

The season for cod's roe is very short, a mere 2–3 weeks between February and March, so it is important to make the most of it. The roes freeze well, either raw or cooked, so it's a good idea to buy extra when they are available. Smaller roes are more delicate in texture, but the larger ones are very good, too.

To cook, simply tie the roe loosely in a plastic bag, cover with boiling water and simmer slowly for 15–20 minutes, until it is firm to the touch. Leave to cool and remove from the bag. The simplest and most traditional preparation is to cut it into thick slices, dip in seasoned flour, or egg and breadcrumbs, and fry gently in a mixture of butter and oil until crisp. Very good indeed for breakfast, with crisp bacon and grilled tomatoes or mushrooms, or for lunch with creamy mashed potato and a slice of lemon.

FOR THE PÂTÉ

110–140 g/4–5 oz cooked cod's roe
55–75 g/2–3 oz butter, melted
juice and grated zest of ½ lemon
salt
pinch of cayenne or chilli pepper to taste
1 tablespoon chopped fresh chives

Purée all the ingredients in a food processor until smooth, seasoning with salt and cayenne or chilli to taste. Pack into individual ramekins and chill. This is delicious served with hot toast, as a starter. If it's not to be eaten for a few hours, cover with melted butter before chilling.

Opposite: *Reaching for Ireland's favourite drink.*

OYSTERS WITH SPICY PORK PATTIES

SERVES 2

St Valentine's Day calls for something with amorous associations: it must be delicious, of course, but not too much trouble. The old fashion of eating chilled oysters and chipolatas (tiny hot spicy sausages) with champagne or white wine seems ideal. Chipolatas may be hard to find, so prepare and chill your own pork patties the day before and then cook them quickly, for a few minutes on each side. Serve hot, alternating with the chilled oysters.

½ onion, finely chopped

1 garlic clove

30 g/1 oz butter

350 g/12 oz lean pork, finely minced

2 teaspoons Yorkshire relish or Worcestershire sauce

a pinch each of dried thyme, grated nutmeg and hot chilli powder

1 tablespoon finely chopped fresh parsley

12 oysters, opened (see note), on the deep half of the shell

Cook the onion and garlic in a little of the butter until soft. If the patties are being prepared in advance, cool, then chill until required.

Mix the meat with the remaining butter, the relish or sauce, seasonings and herbs, then stir in the onion and garlic and mix thoroughly. The mixture should be hot and spicy but not so much that the finished patties kill the taste of the oysters and wine. With floured hands, shape the mixture into small patties, about 4 cm/1½ inches wide. Cook them in a frying pan, without any extra fat, for about 10 minutes.

Note: to open an oyster, hold it firmly in your left hand and insert a short, sharp knife near the hinge, working it from right to left until it begins to release; then prise it open.

POTTED SALMON

SERVES 6 AS A STARTER OR 4 AS A MAIN COURSE

This eighteenth-century Irish recipe, from an old family cookbook, uses ginger, mace, lemon zest and bay leaves. There are no exact measurements. The spices can be adjusted to taste and the quantity of fish available, but the initial salting should be generous. Delicious as a light lunch for 3 or 4 or potted in ramekins, it will serves 6 as a starter. Serve some good bread, triangles of hot toast or crackers alongside.

450 g/1 lb salmon
2 tablespoons sea salt
1 teaspoon ground mace
a pinch of ground ginger
grated zest of 1 lemon
1 bay leaf
110 g/4 oz butter, clarified (see note below)
bread, toast or crackers, to serve

Preheat the oven to 150°C/300°F/Gas Mark 2. Skin and remove the bones from the fish and then cut it into several pieces. Rub all the surfaces well with salt and leave for 3 hours.

Scrape the salt from the fish, wipe with kitchen paper, but don't wash it. Mix together the spices and lemon zest and rub into the fish. Pack the fish into a 600 ml/1 pint oven dish, with the bay leaf on top, and cover with foil. Bake for about 20–30 minutes, or until the fish is cooked. Pour off the juices and remove the bay leaf; then fill the pot up with clarified butter, covering the fish completely. Keep for a day or two before using. To keep for a longer period, 6–7 days, fill the butter up to a depth of 1 cm/½ inch over the top of the fish. Store, well-covered, in the fridge.

Note: to clarify butter, melt the butter gently, then allow it to stand until the sediment falls to the bottom. Carefully pour the clear butter over the fish, leaving the sediment behind.

SMOKED SALMON PÂTÉ

SERVES 6

350 g/12 oz smoked salmon
175 g/6 oz crème fraîche
grated zest and juice of ½ lemon
fresh dill sprigs
75 g/3 oz butter, melted
125 ml/4 fl oz double cream

TO DECORATE
small fresh dill sprigs
gherkins

Skin and chop the salmon, removing any bones or hard pieces. Put in a food processor with the crème fraîche, lemon zest and juice, a few sprigs of dill and 55 g/2 oz of the melted butter. Pulse until the texture you prefer is formed, and then, by hand, gradually beat in the cream.

Rub 6 little ramekins with oil and pack in the pâté. Brush the tops with the remaining butter, cover and chill. To serve, decorate with dill and gherkins. Serve with hot toast or crackers. Serve the pâté in one large bowl if you prefer.

SCOTCH EGGS

SERVES 8 AS A STARTER OR 4 AS A MAIN COURSE

In spite of the name, this combination of pork and eggs has a long and happy history in Ireland. Back in fashion now, Scotch eggs are still in demand for parties and picnics. The mustard mayonnaise really lifts the flavour. Served hot, they're great for lunch or supper too, especially with good buttery mash alongside. Allow one per person, with a few extra. They won't go to waste.

4 eggs
200 g/7 oz pork, very finely minced, or good sausage meat
3 scallions (spring onions), chopped
30 g/1 oz butter
1 tablespoon cornflour
1 tablespoon Worcestershire sauce or soy sauce
1 tablespoon lemon juice
salt and freshly ground black pepper
1 egg yolk
2–3 tablespoons plain flour, for dusting
oil, for deep-frying
crisp lettuce, to serve

FOR THE MUSTARD MAYONNAISE
2 egg yolks, at room temperature
1 tablespoon mild French mustard
300 ml/½ pint olive oil
about 1 tablespoon horseradish cream
salt

Put the eggs into boiling water and cook for 10 minutes exactly, then plunge into cold water to cool.

In a small pan, cook the chopped scallions (spring onions) in the butter until soft. Allow to cool. Mix the pork, scallions, cornflour, Worcestershire or soy sauce, lemon juice, and salt and pepper together to make a paste. Shell the eggs and dry them carefully. Roll in egg yolk, then in flour, shaking off any excess.

Divide the pork into 4 portions and, with floured hands, shape around each egg, encasing them completely. Deep-fry the eggs in sufficient oil to cover, turning frequently to prevent splitting, for about 6–8 minutes until golden brown. Drain on kitchen paper.

For a starter, slice the eggs lengthways and arrange on crisp lettuce. For a picnic, leave them whole.

To make the mustard mayonnaise, beat the egg yolks with the mustard, then slowly pour in the oil, drop by drop at first, and then in a thin stream as it begins to emulsify, stirring continuously, or use an electric beater on medium speed. Season well with a pinch of salt and add creamed horseradish to taste.

Note: should the mayonnaise separate, start again with another egg yolk in a clean bowl and add the mixture, drop by drop, as before.

DEVILLED PRAWNS

SERVES 4 AS A STARTER OR 2 AS A MAIN COURSE

'Devils' – highly spiced morsels of fish or fowl – were hugely popular in Ireland in the past, after dinner, when they were considered a stimulant to the punch bowl, or before dinner, as a spur to jaded appetites. There was great competition for the definitive 'devil' and recipes were constantly exchanged, many of tear-compelling pungency.

12 large raw prawns in their shells
1 teaspoon sea salt
1 teaspoon cayenne pepper
1 teaspoon paprika
1 teaspoon ground cumin
2 tablespoons melted butter
2 limes or 1 lemon
pinch of chilli powder to taste

Peel the body shells from the prawns, but leave the tails intact. To make the 'devil', mix the salt and spices together and form into a paste with the melted butter, the grated zest of 1 lime or ½ lemon and a little juice. To make it hotter, add more cayenne or chilli, but taste constantly. Marinate the prawns in this mixture for a couple of hours in the fridge.

Cook the prawns under a medium grill, turning regularly, until they are just opaque and the tail shells are pink. Slice the remaining lime or lemon and serve the prawns garnished with the citrus slices.

Note: if cooked prawns are used, grill them just sufficiently to heat them through thoroughly.

SMOKED SALMON TARTLETS

These delicate little tartlets, filled with smoked salmon mousse, can be garnished with whatever suits your taste. Try slivers of anchovies with capers, halved quails eggs, or sprigs of fresh dill.

FOR THE PASTRY

280 g/10 oz plain flour
½ teaspoon grated lemon zest
140 g/5 oz butter
1 egg yolk
1 tablespoon very cold water
salt

FOR THE FILLING

225 g/8 oz smoked salmon
240 ml/8 fl oz crème fraîche or double cream,
    or a mixture
2 teaspoons finely chopped fresh dill or tarragon
    or ½ teaspoon dried
½ teaspoon paprika
2 teaspoons lemon juice
1 teaspoon grated lemon zest
a dash of Tabasco or chilli sauce
fresh chervil, tarragon or dill leaves (or other toppings of
    your choice, see above), to garnish

TO SERVE

mixed salad leaves
3–4 tablespoons oil
1–2 tablespoons balsamic vinegar

To make the pastry, sift the flour with a pinch of salt and stir in the lemon zest. Rub in the butter until the mixture resembles breadcrumbs. Moisten with the egg yolk and a tablespoon of cold water and mix to a soft dough. Wrap in cling film and chill for half an hour.

Preheat the oven to 190°C/375°F/Gas Mark 5. Roll out the pastry to fit six 8 cm/3 in buttered tartlet tins. Prick the pastry bottoms. Line with baking parchment and then fit the tins into each other, putting an empty tin (or foil and dried beans) into the top tin. Bake for 15 minutes. Remove from the oven, separate the tins and put back in the oven for a further 4–5 minutes or so until crisp but not too brown. These can be made in advance and kept in a tin. Don't fill them, however, until shortly before serving, so they remain crisp.

Put the salmon and crème fraîche or cream in a food processor, with the herbs, paprika, lemon juice and rind and a dash of Tabasco or chilli sauce. Taste for flavour. Process until a stiff purée is formed and add a little more cream if it's too stiff. Chill until required. Divide the filling between the pastry shells and arrange the garnish of your choice on top.

Whisk together the oil and vinegar to make the dressing. Arrange some salad leaves on each plate and place a tart beside the leaves. Sprinkle a few drops of dressing over the leaves and around the plate.

MUSHROOMS IN PASTRY

SERVES 8 AS A STARTER OR 4 AS A MAIN COURSE

There is a charm in mushrooms that is never quite dispelled by familiarity. Use as many kinds as you can find; their different flavours blend together subtly.

225 g/8 oz spinach
55–75 g/2–3 oz butter
1 garlic clove, finely chopped
450 g/1 lb mixed mushrooms
1 tablespoons mushroom ketchup
    or Worcestershire Sauce
½ teaspoon cayenne pepper
450 g/1 lb frozen or homemade puff pastry
1 egg, beaten
150 ml/¼ pint whipping cream
salt and freshly ground black pepper

Preheat the oven to 190°C/375°F/Gas Mark 5. Wash and coarsely chop the spinach. Melt a knob of butter in a large frying pan and gently cook the garlic for a few moments, and then add the spinach and toss until it is softly wilted. Remove the spinach from the pan and squeeze out any juices back into the pan.

Wipe and trim the mushrooms and chop them coarsely. Add a tablespoon of butter and one of ketchup to the pan and cook the mushrooms until they are reduced but still juicy. Season well with salt, pepper and cayenne. (If oyster mushrooms are used, don't put them in until the last moment.) Remove the mushrooms to cool, but leave the juices in the pan.

Roll out the pastry into 2 large rectangles about 25 x 20 cm/ 10 x 8 inch and leave to rest for 10 minutes. Grease a baking sheet and cover with a sheet of baking parchment. Place one sheet of the pastry on top of the baking sheet and cover with the spinach, leaving a 1 cm/½ inch space around the edges. Pile the mushrooms on top of the spinach and even out. Season well and sprinkle with the cayenne. Dot with the remaining butter, then cover with the other rectangle of pastry, press the dampened edges together and make a vent in the top. Brush with the beaten egg.

Bake until golden, about 40 minutes. Add the cream and remaining butter and bubble for a few minutes to make a sauce.

BLACK PUDDING PATTIES

SERVES 8 AS A STARTER OR 4 AS A MAIN COURSE

Puddings, black and white, are usually eaten at breakfast. These patties make an excellent starter or light lunch.

350 g/12 oz Clonakilty black pudding, or other coarse-textured pudding
225 g/8 oz freshly cooked potato
4 scallions (spring onions), finely chopped
1 large cooking apple, peeled and finely chopped
55 g/2 oz butter
1 egg, beaten
1–2 tablespoons milk (optional)
2 large eating apples
2 tablespoons wholemeal flour
3 tablespoons oil, for frying
small glass of white wine, vermouth or stock
salt and freshly ground black pepper
rocket, watercress or other leaves, to garnish

Peel the casing from the black pudding and finely crumble it into a mixing bowl. Mash in the potato, scallions (spring onions), apple, 30 g/1 oz of the butter and the beaten egg. Season. Mix well, then form into 12 patties, adding a tablespoon or so of milk if the mixture is too dry. Dust with the wholemeal flour and fry gently in the oil until hot and crisp. Keep warm.

Wash the eating apples and cut across into 1 cm/½ inch slices. Stamp out the cores. In a clean pan, fry the apple slices in the remaining butter until beginning to brown but not breaking up. Arrange these on the plates, two per person and put the patties on top. Deglaze the pan with the wine and pour the juices around the patties, garnish with the rocket, watercress or other leaves.

Below: The Conor Pass and Brandon Peak in County Kerry.

OYSTERS IN CHAMPAGNE SAUCE

SERVES 4

*The charm of this dish lies in the combination of the hot sauce
with the cold oysters, the perfect introduction to the Christmas
dinner. The sauce can be made in advance and reheated.*

24 oysters
3 shallots, very finely chopped
30 g/1 oz butter
1½ tablespoons plain flour
a glass of champagne or white wine
300 ml/½ pint cream
cayenne pepper or Tabasco sauce
chopped fresh parsley, to garnish
1 baby gem lettuce, cut into strips
2 lemons, quartered

Scrub the oysters thoroughly and soak them for an hour or so in
cold water. Open the oysters carefully (see below), saving as much
of their liquid as possible, and put them to chill while you make the
sauce. Strain the liquid through a fine sieve.

Cook the shallots and butter in a pan until transparent but not
brown. Add the flour and stir well until it's cooked. Add the
champagne or wine and the strained oyster liquid to the roux,
whisking well to prevent lumps and cooking until reduced
somewhat, about 5 or 6 minutes. Gradually add the cream and
simmer gently until the sauce has reduced and thickened sufficiently.
Season to your taste with the cayenne or Tabasco – it probably
won't need salt.

Just before you are ready to serve, arrange the oysters in their shells
onto plates and put a spoonful of the hot sauce over each cold
oyster. Garnish with the parsley, lettuce and lemon wedges.

Note: to open an oyster, hold it firmly in your left hand and insert
a short sharp knife near the hinge, working it from right to left until
the muscle is severed; then prise the oyster open.

SMOKED FISH TART WITH ARDRAHAN CHEESE

SERVES 6 AS A STARTER OR 4 AS A MAIN COURSE

Ardrahan is a semi-soft cheese with a pungent aroma, from Kanturk, Co. Cork. Combining it with smoked fish is the inspirational idea of Geert Maes, chef patron of Gaby's Restaurant in Killarney, one of Ireland's most respected restaurants. Here it is partnered with smoked haddock, to make a simple but delicious tart.

FOR THE PASTRY

110 g/4 oz butter

200 g/7 oz plain flour

¼ teaspoon salt

1 egg yolk

1–2 tablespoons very cold water, if necessary

FOR THE FILLING

1 onion, chopped

1 carrot, chopped

½ tablespoon oil

1 bay leaf

½ teaspoon black peppercorns

225 g/8 oz smoked haddock or cod

110 g/4 oz Ardrahan cheese (or other semi-soft cheese with a mature flavour)

4 large eggs

300 ml/½ pint cream

freshly ground black pepper and grated nutmeg

Preheat the oven to 200°C/400°F/Gas Mark 6. To make the pastry, rub the butter into the sifted flour and salt, moisten with the egg yolk, adding a tablespoon or so of cold water if required to knead gently to a soft dough. Roll out, or press into a 23 x 5 cm/ 9 x 3 inch quiche tin. Chill until required.

Gently fry the chopped onion and carrot in the oil until soft, then add the bay leaf and peppercorns and enough water just to cover. Boil for about 10 minutes. Gently poach the fish in this stock until cooked, 5–6 minutes. Take out the fish, flake and remove any bones or hard pieces. Strain the stock and keep it for soups.

With a potato peeler, remove the thin outer rind from the Ardrahan cheese and then cut the cheese into thin slices. Arrange these on the base of the pastry and put the flaked fish on top.

Beat the eggs and cream together and season well with black pepper and a pinch of nutmeg. It probably won't need salt. Pour into the pastry and bake for 5 minutes, then turn the oven temperature down to 150°C/300°F/Gas Mark 2 and cook for a further 35 minutes until golden on top and the pastry has shrunk slightly away from the sides of the tin.

Opposite: Forest mosses at Skellig Michael in County Kerry.

BAKED EGGS WITH SPINACH

4 large eggs, at room temperature
225 g/8 oz spinach
1 tablespoon butter, plus extra for greasing
2 streaky bacon rashers
a few drops of soy sauce
150 ml/¼ pint double cream
salt and freshly ground black pepper
chopped fresh chervil

Preheat the oven to 180°C/350°F/Gas Mark 4. Wash the spinach and remove the stalks. Chop coarsely, place in a pan with a knob of butter and simmer gently until just tender. Squeeze out the moisture. Grill the bacon until crisp and then chop finely.

Butter four individual ramekins. Put a tablespoon of spinach in each, sprinkle the bacon over it and season well, adding a drop or two of soy sauce to each ramekin. Crack the eggs into the ramekins and cover with the cream. Sprinkle the chervil over the top. Bake for 12–15 minutes until the egg whites are set and the yolks still soft.

Above: Michael's Stone Steps, Skellig, County Kerry.

SOUPS

SPRING GREEN SOUP

SERVES 6

Give yourself a spring boost with this green soup using the early shoots of nutrient-rich herbs. Vary the ingredients according to what can be foraged or found in the shops.

large handful of sorrel leaves
large handful of spinach
handful of young nettles or dandelion leaves
heart of a small green cabbage
55 g/2 oz butter
2 onions, finely chopped
2 garlic cloves, chopped
chopped fresh thyme
2 potatoes, peeled and chopped
1 litre/1¾ pints chicken stock, or milk and water
150 ml/¼ pint whipping cream
salt and freshly ground black pepper

Wash all the leaves thoroughly in salted water, removing any coarse stalks or ribs. Keep the nettles separate. Prepare the cabbage in the same way, shake dry and finely chop.

Melt the butter in a large saucepan and gently sweat the onions, garlic, spinach, cabbage, sorrel and thyme. Add the potatoes and the stock, or milk and water, and simmer until the potato is soft. Then add the nettles and cook until they are tender, about 30 minutes. Liquidise, add the cream, adjust the seasoning and serve.

Previous page: Evening at Lough Gill, County Sligo.

SPICY CARROT SOUP

1 tablespoon oil
1 tablespoon mustard seeds
30 g/1 oz butter
2 medium onions, chopped
4–5 large carrots, grated
1 tablespoon coriander seeds
1.2 litres/2 pints chicken or vegetable stock
2 tablespoons porridge oats
3 teaspoons cider vinegar
juice and grated zest of 1 large orange
salt and freshly ground black pepper
whipping cream, to garnish (optional)
chopped fresh coriander, to garnish (optional)

Heat the oil in a large saucepan and add the mustard seeds, heating until they pop. Add the butter and onions and cook on a low heat until they begin to soften. Then add the carrots and coriander seeds and continue cooking for 5–6 minutes. Add half the stock and the porridge oats and cook a further few minutes.

If you like a smooth soup, purée the mixture at this point. Return it to the saucepan, add the vinegar, orange juice and zest and the remaining stock. Season well with salt and pepper, simmer for a few moments and serve.

The soup can be garnished with a swirl of cream and some chopped, fresh coriander.

POTATO SOUP WITH SALMON AND CHIVES

SERVES 6

This rather unusual potato soup uses the excellent farmed salmon that is available all year round.

175 g/6 oz salmon, cutlet or tail piece
55 g/2 oz butter
1 onion, finely chopped
2 leeks, chopped
6 medium potatoes, peeled and chopped
1 bay leaf
600 ml/1 pint chicken or fish stock
600 ml/1 pint milk
2 tablespoons finely chopped fresh chives
salt and freshly ground black pepper
Wholemeal Scones (see page 148) and butter, to serve

Put the salmon in a small saucepan, just barely cover with water, and poach gently until the fish is cooked, about 10 minutes. Remove from the water, skin, remove bones and flake. Use the water to make up the stock.

Melt the butter in a large saucepan and cook the onion and leeks until tender but not coloured. Add the potatoes, bay leaf, seasoning and the stock, and cook until the potatoes are soft. Remove the bay leaf, then purée in a food processor. Return to the saucepan. Next add the milk, chives and salmon and heat through gently. Adjust the seasoning and serve hot. Wholemeal scones with butter turn this soup into a little feast.

Opposite: Sunset over Lough Gill.

CRAB SOUP WITH SAFFRON

SERVES 6

4–5 saffron strands
6 large scallions (spring onions), finely chopped
1 garlic clove
2 teaspoons fresh marjoram
30 g/1 oz butter
900 ml/1½ pints fish or light chicken stock
1 tablespoon long-grain rice
1 tablespoon grated lemon zest
350 g/12 oz cooked crab meat
150 ml/¼ pint whipping cream
salt and freshly ground black pepper
1 tablespoon chopped fresh parsley, to garnish

Soak the saffron in a little water for 30 minutes. Cook the finely chopped scallions (spring onions), garlic and marjoram in the butter until soft. Add the stock, rice, lemon zest and saffron, with its water, and simmer gently until the rice is soft. Add the crab and the cream and season well. Bring to the boil very gently, simmer for 2–3 minutes until hot, garnish with the parsley and serve.

LOVAGE SOUP

Lovage, once to be found in many Irish gardens, has celery-like leaves that make interesting soups and salads. Celery leaves are delicious prepared in the same way.

2–3 large handfuls of young lovage leaves, chopped
30 g/1 oz butter
1 onion
1 garlic clove
1 tablespoon lemon juice, plus extra to taste
1 tablespoon plain flour
600 ml/1 pint hot chicken stock
600 ml/1 pint milk
salt and freshly ground black pepper
4 tablespoons croûtons

Melt the butter in a large saucepan and cook the onion and garlic until soft. Add the chopped lovage and lemon juice. Cook until the leaves soften a little and then sprinkle in the flour. Continue stirring until the flour is cooked and the mixture is smooth. Gradually add half the hot stock, little by little, stirring well, until the soup has thickened and the sorrel has cooked. Purée in a food processor or blender until smooth.

Return the soup to the saucepan, add the rest of the stock and the milk and bring back to the boil. Season well with plenty of black pepper and salt to taste. Just before serving sprinkle the croûtons over the top.

Note: to make the croûtons, remove the crusts from 3 slices of white bread, cut into cubes and fry in a little oil, until brown. Drain on kitchen paper.

PEA POD SOUP

The pods of baby peas, so juicy and sweet, make very good soup, with an intense pea taste. Sugar-snap peas, now readily available, give something of the same flavour.

225 g/8 oz sugar-snap peas
1 onion, finely chopped
30 g/1 oz butter
30 g/1 oz plain flour
750 ml/1¼ pints hot chicken or vegetable stock
1 teaspoon roughly chopped summer savory or fresh mint
½ teaspoon sugar
1 tablespoon chopped fresh parsley
salt and freshly ground black pepper
3–4 tablespoons whipping cream
chopped fresh savory or mint, to garnish

Wash the peas, put them in a large saucepan and just cover with water. Simmer gently until the peas are just tender, about 15 minutes. Strain the peas and keep the water. In a large saucepan, cook the onion in the butter until soft. Mix in the flour and keep stirring until cooked, 2–3 minutes. Gradually add half the hot stock, stirring well until it thickens and the flour is cooked. Add the savory or mint. Blitz this mixture, with the peas, with a hand blender or food processor and process until smooth, then return it to the pan.

Add the remainder of the stock, the sugar, parsley, salt and pepper. Check the seasoning and bring to the boil for 2–3 minutes. A little of the pea water can be added for a thinner soup. Serve in small bowls with a swirl of cream in each bowl. Garnish with savory or mint.

WALNUT SOUP WITH WALNUT AND CRESS SANDWICHES

SERVES 4

This simple soup is best made in the winter, when the new season's nuts are fresh. Good homemade stock will also greatly add to the flavour. This soup is particularly popular with men – perhaps because it was frequently served in conjunction with game.

110 g/4 oz shelled walnuts
1 large garlic clove
675 g/1¼ pints chicken stock
300 ml/½ pint whipping cream
grated nutmeg
salt and freshly ground black pepper
1 tablespoon finely chopped fresh chives or parsley, to garnish

FOR THE SANDWICHES
110 g/4 oz cream cheese
2 tablespoons finely chopped walnuts
2–3 tablespoons chopped cress or flat-leaved parsley
6–8 slices of thinly sliced pan loaf, preferably brown or homemade

To make the soup, crush or blend the walnuts and garlic to a smooth paste, adding a little stock to help it along. Blend in the rest of the stock, add the cream and season well, grating a very little nutmeg over it. Bring to the boil and simmer gently for 4–6 minutes before serving. Garnish with the herbs.

Make the sandwich filling by beating together the cream cheese, walnuts and cress. Remove the crusts from the pan loaf, make the sandwiches and cut into quarters to serve.

CHESTNUT AND LENTIL SOUP

SERVES 6

With its warm colour and earthy flavours, this lovely soup is redolent of autumn. Try a glass of not-too-dry sherry – an amontillado, perhaps, which is delicious with the soup; it's a fashion that is due for revival.

2 streaky bacon rashers, finely chopped
2 large onions, finely chopped
2 garlic cloves, finely chopped
55 g/2 oz butter
3 celery sticks, with leaves, chopped
1 carrot, grated
225 g/8 oz chestnut purée (homemade or bought)
175 g/6 oz green or brown lentils
1 teaspoon ground cumin
1.2 litres/2 pints chicken or vegetable stock
150 ml/¼ pint whipping cream, to serve (optional)
salt and freshly ground black pepper

Put the bacon, onions and garlic in a large saucepan with the butter and sauté until the bacon is crisp and the onions are soft. Add the chopped celery (reserve the leaves) and carrot and cook for 3–4 minutes. Stir in the chestnut purée. Add the lentils, cumin and the stock and simmer gently until the lentils are soft.

Reserve 1–2 cupfuls of the soup to give a little texture, and purée the remainder. Return to the reserved soup and check the seasoning. Reheat before swirling a spoonful of cream in each bowl, if using, then scatter the chopped celery leaves over the top.

CELERY SOUP WITH BLUE CHEESE

SERVES 6

1 large head of celery

2 garlic cloves

1 onion

30 g/1 oz butter

30 g/1 oz plain flour

1.2 litres/2 pints vegetable or light chicken stock

150 ml/¼ pint whipping cream

a little milk, if necessary

55–75 g/2–3 oz Cashel Blue cheese, crumbled,
   or other semi-hard blue cheese

2–3 scallions (spring onions), finely chopped, to garnish

salt and freshly ground black pepper

crusty bread, to serve

Prepare and finely chop the celery, garlic and onion. Melt the butter in a large saucepan, add the prepared vegetables and stir frequently until they begin to soften. Sift in the flour and stir well until it has cooked. Gradually add the hot stock, mixing well to avoid lumps. Cook for 10 minutes or so until the vegetables are completely cooked, and then put through the blender.

Return the soup to the saucepan, season well and add the cream. (If it seems too thick, add a little milk also.) Cook for a few moments to amalgamate the cream.

Just before serving, bring back to the boil and stir in the crumbled cheese, but don't continue to boil once it has been added. Garnish with the finely chopped scallions (spring onions). Serve with plenty of crusty bread.

MAINS

HAKE BAKED IN PAPER

SERVES 4

This method of cooking was widely used in the past to protect delicate morsels from the heat of the open fire. Writing paper was often specified in the recipes. Baking parchment, however is the ideal material, sealing in the flavours and appearing somehow more aesthetic on the plate than foil. Serve with a selection of roasted vegetables (see note).

4 hake fillets, weighing 110–225 g/4–8 oz each
55 g/2 oz butter
1 large red pepper
few sprigs fresh dill or marjoram
4 tablespoons dry vermouth or white wine
8–10 live mussels, scrubbed and bearded, to garnish
salt and freshly ground black pepper

Preheat the oven to 180°C/350°F/Gas Mark 4.

Cut 4 pieces of baking parchment large enough to enclose the pieces of fish. Season and butter the fish well and place one on each piece of parchment. Slice the pepper into thin rounds, removing any seeds or white membrane, and place one or two slices on top of each piece of fish. Sprinkle a a sprig or two of dill or marjoram on each and pour on a tablespoon of vermouth or wine. Bring the two sides of the paper together and pleat lengthways, tucking the ends firmly under the packet to seal.

Place the fish parcels in a baking dish and bake for about 20–25 minutes, depending on the thickness of the fillets. Steam the mussels open in a covered pan with a few tablespoons of water. Discard any that don't open. When the fish is ready, cut a slit in the paper with scissors, slide in the mussels and herbs and serve.

Note: a mixture of seasonal vegetables, such as red and green peppers, celery, shallots and courgettes, can be brushed with olive oil and roasted in the oven at the same time. Include some unpeeled cloves of garlic and sprigs of thyme. Cut the vegetables into equal-size pieces and put them into the oven about 20 minutes before the fish goes in. They take about 40 minutes to cook in a hot oven.

Previous page: Slea Head and Coumeenoole Beach, County Kerry.

SALMON CAKES WITH DILL SAUCE

To make these fish cakes, use either a tail piece or cutlets or, better still, the buttery remains of a whole salmon.

675 g/1½ lb salmon
3 tablespoons finely chopped shallot
75 g/3 oz butter, melted
1 egg yolk
1 tablespoon lemon juice
1 tablespoon finely chopped fresh herbs
140 g/5 oz breadcrumbs
1 tablespoon whipped cream, if necessary
1 egg, beaten
2 tablespoons each wholemeal flour and breadcrumbs, mixed
salt and freshly ground black pepper
oil and butter, for frying
fresh green salad, to serve

FOR THE DILL SAUCE
1 tablespoon butter
1 tablespoon plain flour
240 ml/8 fl oz hot milk
3–4 tablespoons crème fraîche
2 tablespoons finely chopped fresh dill or 2 teaspoons dried dill
salt and freshly ground black pepper

Poach the salmon in lightly salted water for 12–15 minutes. Remove any skin and bones and flake the fish. Sauté the shallot in a little of the butter until soft.

Mix the salmon, shallot, egg yolk, lemon juice, all but 1 tablespoon of the melted butter, the herbs and seasoning together. Add the 140 g/5 oz of breadcrumbs and work well together. Add a spoonful of cream if the mixture is too dry. Flour the hands well, then shape into 4 or 8 cakes, patting them firmly into shape. Dip into the beaten egg and then into the breadcrumb and flour mixture to coat.

Melt the remaining butter and oil in a large frying-pan and cook the cakes for 5–6 minutes on each side until crisp and very hot.

Meanwhile, to make the sauce, melt the butter in a saucepan, whisk in the flour and stir until cooked, about a minute. Off the heat, gradually whisk in the hot milk. Bring back to the boil and stir until the sauce thickens. Remove from the heat, add the crème fraîche and dill and season to taste.

Drain the salmon cakes on kitchen paper and serve with the dill sauce and a green salad.

BUTTER BEAN HOT POT

SERVES 4–5

This is the kind of warming, comforting supper we all love to come home to.

225 g/8 oz butter beans, soaked overnight
oil, for frying
450 g/1 lb onions, sliced
450 g/1 lb piece of bacon, streaky or collar cut, cubed
450 g/1 lb sharp cooking apples, peeled and sliced
450 g/1 lb potatoes, sliced
chopped fresh thyme
1 or 2 fresh sage leaves
300 ml/½ pint stock or water
salt and freshly ground black pepper

Drain the beans, cover with fresh water, bring to the boil and boil for 10 minutes, then simmer gently until almost soft but not breaking up, about 40 minutes.

Preheat the oven to 150°C/300°F/Gas Mark 2. Brown the meat in a little oil in a heavy pan. Remove the meat, then brown the onions in the same pan. Layer the onions, bacon, apples, potatoes and beans in a greased ovenproof casserole, sprinkling with pepper and thyme and tucking in the sage leaves. Finish with a layer of potatoes. Add a very little salt, lots of black pepper and pour the stock over everything. Cover with foil or a lid, and bake for about 1½ hours.

Remove the foil and continue cooking until the potatoes are brown. Add a little more stock, if necessary. A simple green salad is all you need with this.

Above: Slea Head ruins, County Kerry.

FRICASSÉE OF PORK

SERVES 6

1 large onion, chopped
30 g/1 oz butter
1 tablespoon oil
350 g/12 oz button mushrooms
900 g/2 lb boneless pork, cubed
1 tablespoon plain flour
2 teaspoons ground cumin
150 ml/¼ pint dry white wine or stock
300 ml/½ pint whipping cream
2 celery sticks, thinly sliced
salt and freshly ground black pepper

Below: Portmagee Village, County Kerry.

Preheat the oven to 150°C/300°F/Gas Mark 2. Soften the onion in half the butter and oil, then transfer to an ovenproof dish. Add the mushrooms to the pan and cook for a few minutes until lightly browned. Pour, with any juice, into the dish. Toss the cubed pork in the flour and cumin and brown in the pan with the remaining oil and butter. Add to the dish. Sprinkle any remaining flour into the pan and stir for a few moments to cook. Add the wine or stock, scraping up all the sediment thoroughly. Now add the cream, check and adjust the seasoning and stir well.

Pour over the pork mixture, stir in the thinly sliced celery, cover and cook gently until the pork is tender, 45–60 minutes. Serve with creamy mashed potatoes, rice or noodles.

CHICKEN AND CHEESE WRAPPED IN BACON

SERVES 4

Cashel Blue cheese, from Tipperary and widely available in cheese shops, gives just the right note of acidity to the chicken.

4 boneless, skinless chicken breasts
8 rindless streaky bacon rashers
2–3 fresh sage leaves, torn
1 teaspoon grated lemon zest
175 g/6 oz Cashel Blue cheese
30 g/1 oz butter
a glass of white wine, vermouth or chicken stock
2–3 tablespoons whipping cream
salt and freshly ground black pepper
crisp green salad or fresh vegetables, to serve

TO GARNISH
lemon wedges
fresh sage leaves

Place a chicken breast flat on a board and, with a sharp knife, slice in two horizontally. Cover each piece with clingfilm and beat gently with a rolling pin until slightly larger. Cut each bacon rasher in two and stretch them out by stroking with the blade of a large knife. Lay two pieces of bacon side by side on the board, put a small piece of sage on top and cover with a piece of chicken. Season the chicken well and sprinkle with lemon zest.

Cut the cheese into 8 fingers and place one on each piece of chicken, roll up the bacon and chicken and secure with cocktail sticks or thread. Continue with the rest of the bacon and chicken until you have 8 rolls. In a heavy pan, brown the rolls in the butter, turning frequently, for about 10 minutes until the chicken is cooked and the cheese is beginning to melt.

Transfer the rolls to a hot dish and remove the cocktail sticks. Add the wine, vermouth or stock to the pan, scraping up all the sediment, and bubbling well for a few moments to reduce the wine. Add the cream, bubble again for 2–3 minutes, then check and adjust the seasoning. Pour a little sauce onto the centre of each plate and arrange the rolls on top.

Garnish with lemon wedges and a few sage leaves. Serve with a crisp salad or a green vegetable.

Opposite: Ogham Stones, Kilmalkader, County Kerry.

SPRING LAMB CUTLETS IN PASTRY

SERVES 4

Easter is the time of renewal and lamb symbolises the return of life in many cultures. Roast baby lamb is the traditional Easter Sunday dinner and is pure magic, especially when it's moist and tender and delicately pink. As a change from the usual leg of lamb, try this rack of lamb in pastry, a great party dish and very easy to carve – simply cut down between the cutlet bones. You will need 2 cutlets per person, possibly 3 if they are very tiny. This sauce is invariably served with lamb in Ireland and it's very much an eighteenth-century idea, the vinegar counteracting the fattiness of the meat.

1 rack of lamb (about 8 cutlets)
450 g/1 lb puff pastry
55 g/2 oz butter
4 shallots, finely chopped
225 g/8 oz mushrooms, finely chopped
110 g/4 oz dried apricots, finely chopped
1 tablespoon chopped fresh mint or oregano
1 egg, beaten, to glaze
½ tablespoon grated lemon zest and 1 tablespoon juice
salt and freshly ground black pepper

FOR THE MINT SAUCE
1–2 tablespoons chopped fresh mint
1–2 tablespoons sugar, or to taste
1–2 tablespoons cider or white wine vinegar
3–4 tablespoons water

Preheat the oven to 220°C/425°F/Gas Mark 7. Rub the lamb with half the butter and season well. Roast the meat for 8–10 minutes, depending on the size of the cutlets. Allow to cool completely.

Gently cook the shallots, mushrooms, apricots and mint or oregano in the remaining butter until the juices have thickened. Season this well with lemon zest, lemon juice and plenty of black pepper. Press the stuffing between the cutlets. Roll out the pastry into a sheet large enough to enclose the rack and fold around the meat, allowing the bones to stick out through the pastry. Cover these with foil to prevent them from burning.

Decorate with pastry trimmings. Wash over the pastry with the beaten egg. Heat the oven to 180°C/350°F/Gas Mark 4 and bake until the pastry is browned, about 25–30 minutes.

Meanwhile, to make the sauce, bring all the ingredients to the boil, then remove from the heat, stirring to dissolve the sugar. Allow to cool. More or less mint can be added and apple jelly can be used instead of the sugar, if you prefer. Serve the lamb with the mint sauce.

IRISH STEW

There is much argument concerning the authentic Irish stew, but for most of us, I suspect, the 'authentic' dish is the one made in our own families. The pure tradition uses only mutton, potatoes, onion, thyme and seasoning, and this, I think, is generally agreed to be the thing. In my home, barley was included and some contemporary recipes include carrots, and even celery, so you can make your own choice.

450 g/1 lb onions
1.15 kg/2½ lb potatoes
900 g/2 lb neck of lamb chops
30 g/1 oz butter
2 carrots, chopped
2 celery sticks, chopped
1 large fresh thyme sprig
450 ml/¾ pint water or lamb stock
salt and white pepper

Chop the onions coarsely. Peel and slice the potatoes thickly. Season the chops well with salt and pepper.

Put the butter in the bottom of a heavy saucepan and then layer the meat and vegetables, finishing with a layer of potatoes. Bury the thyme in the centre. Pour in the stock or water. Cover the pan tightly with foil and a lid, bring to the boil and then immediately lower the heat and cook gently on the lowest possible heat for about 1½ hours. The meat and vegetables should cook in their juices with very little liquid left at the end, so watch for burning. It may be necessary to add more liquid.

Note: the stew can also be cooked in the oven and if barley is included it's less likely to burn in the oven.

CORNED BEEF AND CABBAGE

SERVES 6–8

'Corned' beef, an old word for pickled beef, can be prepared at home using the method for Spiced Beef, leaving out the spices.

1.3–1.8 kg/3–4 lb beef brisket (prepared as p.84)

2 carrots, coarsely chopped
2 celery sticks, coarsely chopped
1 onion, coarsely chopped
1 tablespoon brown sugar
1 tablespoon mustard powder
2–3 cloves
1 green or savoy cabbage
boiled potatoes with butter and mustard, to serve

Prepare the beef as for Spiced Beef (see page 84) and leave to pickle for 10 days in the fridge, turning from time to time, then drain the meat, discarding the pickle, and pat dry. If you are buying shop-pickled beef, soak the meat for several hours in cold water.

When ready to cook, put the meat with the vegetables and seasonings, except the cabbage, into a large saucepan. Cover with cold water and bring it to the boil very slowly. Simmer gently for about 2 hours (20 minutes per 450 g/1 lb). When the meat is tender, turn off the heat and rest it in the water for 30 minutes, while you prepare the cabbage.

Wash and quarter the cabbage and put in a large saucepan with a ladleful of the cooking water from the meat. Pour in enough boiling water to cover half the depth of the cabbage. Boil hard, without a lid, until the cabbage is just tender. Drain and keep warm while you slice the beef. Arrange the meat on a deep dish and put the cabbage around it.

The traditional method is to put the cabbage into the pot with the meat for the last 15 minutes cooking time, but I feel the rather lean meat benefits from a resting period and the cabbage is less greasy when cooked on its own.

Serve with mustard and plain boiled potatoes, and of course, plenty of butter for the spuds.

CHICKEN AND HAM PASTIES

MAKES 4

These traditional pasties are ideal 'prepare ahead' food for summer eating. Pair them with salads and chutney, or baby new potatoes for lunches and family dinners, or pack them in boxes for days at the beach.

2 small leeks, finely chopped

100 g/3½ oz mushrooms, sliced

55 g/2 oz butter

1 tablespoon plain flour

300 ml/½ pint hot milk

¼ teaspoon coriander seeds

225 g/8 oz cooked chicken, finely chopped

225 g/8 oz cooked ham, finely chopped

1 teaspoon poppy seeds

salt and freshly ground black pepper

FOR THE PASTRY

400 g/14 oz plain flour

225 g/8 oz butter

1 small egg, beaten, to glaze

salt, pinch

Preheat the oven to 190°C/375°F/Gas Mark 5.

Make the pastry in the usual way by rubbing the butter into the flour and salt and moistening with 2–4 tablespoons of cold water, then roll it out and cut into four 15 cm/6 inch circles. Chill while you make the filling.

Sauté the leeks with the mushrooms in 30 g/1 oz butter. Set aside. Melt the remaining butter in a saucepan, stir in the flour, and cook for 2–3 minutes. Gradually add the hot milk, stirring continuously until the sauce thickens smoothly. Season well. Add the coriander seeds and the leek mixture and its juices. Cool completely.

Fold the finely chopped meats into the sauce and divide among the pastry circles. Dampen the edges with a little of the beaten egg, then draw up the 2 sides together, pinching well to seal. Place, seam-side down, on a greased baking sheet. Brush with the remaining beaten egg and sprinkle with poppy seeds. Bake until the pastry is golden, 20–25 minutes.

MACKEREL WITH GOOSEBERRY SAUCE

SERVES 6

This is a combination that has its origins in the past, when fruit sauces with fish or meat were considered good for the digestion. Apple sauce with pork is another example. The elderflowers give a delicate muscatel flavour and were often added to apple and gooseberry tarts. Pick the elderflowers well away from dusty roadsides. The sauce can be either hot or cold and it's equally good with kippers or pork.

6 mackerel, scaled and cleaned

2 tablespoons plain flour

1 egg, beaten

3 tablespoons fine oatmeal

butter and oil, for frying

salt and freshly ground black pepper

baby new potatoes and finely chopped scallions
  (spring onions), to serve

FOR THE GOOSEBERRY SAUCE

450 g/1 lb gooseberries

1–2 heads of elderflowers

2–3 tablespoons water

sugar, to taste

To make the sauce, gently cook the gooseberries and elderflowers with 2–3 tablespoons of water until soft. Remove the elderflowers, sweeten to taste and push through a sieve. Set aside.

Clean the mackerel, wash and dry, removing heads if preferred. Season the insides and flour well. Dip the mackerel in the beaten egg, then roll in the oatmeal. Melt a tablespoon each of butter and oil in a large non-stick frying-pan and fry the mackerel over a low heat until the flesh is opaque. Drain on kitchen paper and serve with the gooseberry sauce.

This is great with baby new potatoes, perked up with finely chopped scallions (spring onions) and lots of black pepper.

BAKED SALMON WITH A HERB CRUST

SERVES 6–7

For maximum effect and not too much effort, this baked salmon has it all. Ask your fishmonger to split your fish lengthways into two long fillets. A 1.3 kg/3lb fish will be enough for 6 with side dishes.

1.3–2.25 kg/3–5 lb salmon prepared into 2 filleted sides
2.5 cm/1 inch cube of fresh root ginger
6 tinned anchovies, drained
110 g/4 oz butter
3 tablespoons finely chopped fresh parsley
3 tablespoons finely chopped scallions (spring onions)
grated zest of 1 lemon
75 g/3 oz breadcrumbs, made from day-old bread

FOR THE SAUCE

3 egg yolks
300 ml/½ pint whipping cream
5–6 sorrel leaves, ribs removed, leaves chopped
grated zest of 1 lemon
1 tablespoon fresh chopped coriander or parsley
salt and freshly ground black pepper

Preheat the oven to 160°C/325°F/Gas Mark 3.

Mash the ginger to a paste with the anchovies, 75 g/3 oz of the butter, the parsley, scallions (spring onions) and grated zest of half the lemon. Butter a sheet of baking parchment which will fit the salmon and line a large baking tray. Lay one fillet of salmon on the paper, skin-side down, and spread with half the herb butter. Lay the other fillet on top, skin-side up, reversing the wide end over the narrow end of the bottom fillet. Spread the remaining herb butter on top. Cover the salmon with the breadcrumbs, patting them down lightly; season well and dot with the remaining butter. Bake in the oven for 12 minutes per 450 g/1 lb.

Meanwhile, make the sauce. Season the egg yolks and beat together. Bring the cream to the boil, with the sorrel leaves and lemon zest and cook to reduce for a few moments. Cool slightly, then pour slowly on to the yolks, stirring all the time. Return to the saucepan and over a low heat, cook, stirring continuously and without allowing it to boil, until the sauce thickens slightly.

When the fish is cooked, use the baking paper to lift the fish on to a heated serving dish and strain the buttery fish juices into the sauce. Add the coriander or parsley and serve.

Note: If the sauce shows signs of becoming lumpy, scrape immediately into a mini-blender and blitz for a few seconds.

SCALLOPS WITH TARRAGON SAUCE

SERVES 6 AS A STARTER, DEPENDING ON THE SIZE OF THE SCALLOPS, OR 3–4 AS A MAIN COURSE

Tender, juicy scallops need very little cooking. Be sure to save the red corals when cleaning them.

175 ml/6 fl oz white wine
100 ml/3 fl oz water
grated zest and juice of ½ lemon
4–5 fresh tarragon leaves or a pinch of dried tarragon
12 scallops, cleaned
100 ml/3 fl oz cream
1 tablespoon butter
3 egg yolks, beaten
1 tablespoon finely chopped fresh parsley
mixed baby salad leaves, to garnish
2 teaspoons paprika
dressed salad, to serve

Below: Slea Head and Blasket Islands, Dingle Peninsula, County Kerry.

Put the wine, water, lemon juice and zest and tarragon leaves together in a saucepan and boil for 2–3 minutes. Add the scallops and corals and gently poach for 3–5 minutes, depending on size, until they are no longer translucent and just firm to the touch. Remove to a warm place.

Strain the cooking liquid into a small saucepan and boil rapidly, to reduce slightly. Add the cream and butter and simmer for 5–6 minutes. Now pour slowly on to the egg yolks, whisking well as you pour. Return the mixture to the saucepan over a very low heat and continue to stir until the sauce thickens slightly, being careful not to let it boil. Season well, add the parsley and more tarragon to taste.

Arrange the scallops on warm plates and pour the sauce over them. Add a little pile of dressed salad leaves to each plate and finish with a dusting of paprika.

HAM IN PASTRY

SERVES 10 AS A MAIN COURSE OR 25 AS PART OF A PARTY SUPPER

Hams, and the art of cooking them, are well understood in Ireland and they are always popular for grand occasions. If the ham is to be eaten hot, seasonal vegetables and a well-made parsley sauce are the traditional partners. Rowanberry jelly or redcurrant jelly heated with a glass of port and a little orange juice, also makes an excellent sauce.

2.8–3.6 kg/6–8 lb fillet of ham
juniper berries
2 bay leaves
1 large onion, halved
2–3 tablespoons brown sugar
1 tablespoon mustard powder
900 g/2 lb puff or shortcrust pastry
2 tablespoons Dijon-type mild mustard
1 egg, beaten, to glaze

Soak the ham overnight in cold water if it seems to be salty; otherwise 1–2 hours will do.

When ready to cook, put the ham in a large saucepan, with a few juniper berries, the bay leaves and the onion halves. Add the sugar and mustard powder, cover with cold water, then bring to the boil slowly and, timing from when the water boils, simmer for 20 minutes per 450 g/1 lb. Test before the last 20 minutes, as it may not be necessary because the ham will cook a little more in the oven. When cooked, allow to cool for about 30 minutes in the water, then remove and peel off the skin and some of the fat if there is too much. Allow the ham to cool further.

Preheat the oven to 190°C/375°F/Gas Mark 5. Roll out the pastry into a large square that will cover the ham, keeping it a little thicker than usual. Rub Dijon mustard over the ham and then drape the pastry over the ham, cover it completely, tucking the pastry underneath, trimming the surplus and dampening and sealing the joins. Place on a baking tray, keeping the seams underneath as far as possible. Brush over with the beaten egg. Use the trimmings to make leaves etc. and brush over with the egg again. Make a vent at the highest point.

Bake for about 20 minutes. If serving the ham hot, cover the pastry loosely with foil, lower the heat to 160°C/325°F/Gas Mark 3 for another 45 minutes or so, to ensure the ham is completely heated through.

JELLIED TONGUE

SERVES 6 AS A MAIN COURSE OR 8–10 AS PART OF A PARTY SUPPER

Liked and disliked with equal intensity, a pressed pickled tongue is an essential ingredient of any Irish cold meat platter and, though it takes a long time to cook, the preparation is extremely simple. A little port added to the stock gives a zing to the jelly. Small, ready-trimmed tongues are widely available and usually don't need to be soaked; larger tongues may need soaking overnight.

1 tongue, weighing about 900 g/2 lb
1 onion
1 carrot
1 celery stick
1 or 2 cloves or ½ star anise
2 teaspoons black peppercorns
1 orange
4 teaspoons/11 g or ½ oz sachet/3 leaves gelatine
a glass of port
spicy Cumberland sauce or horseradish sauce, to serve

Place the tongue in a large saucepan and cover with cold water. Add the vegetables, cloves, peppercorns and a large strip of orange zest. Bring to the boil very slowly and simmer gently until a skewer will slide in easily. This can take from 2–4 hours, depending on its size. Remove the tongue from the water when cool enough to handle and peel off the skin and any gristle. Return the tongue to the stock, to keep warm.

Strain off 300 ml/½ pint of the cooking liquid and use a little to dissolve the gelatine, according to the packet directions. Put the remainder in a small saucepan, with the port and the juice of ½ the orange. Boil hard to reduce for 1–2 minutes; cool slightly, then add the dissolved gelatine. Put the warm tongue in a bowl or mould that will just hold it. Pour over enough of the port jelly to cover it when it is pressed down well with a plate or saucer. Put a weight on top of the plate (tin cans or a stone) and leave overnight. Set aside any remaining port jelly to set, for the garnish.

To serve, remove any fat from the top, turn out the tongue and carve in thin slices. Decorate with the chopped jelly. Spicy Cumberland sauce or horseradish cream can be served with it.

RAGOUT OF SCALLOPS AND BACON

SERVES 4

8 large scallops, cleaned

30 g/1 oz butter

4 streaky bacon rashers

1 onion, chopped

2–3 scallions (spring onions), chopped

225 g/8 oz mixed shiitake and oyster mushrooms

2 teaspoons plain flour

150 ml/¼ pint white wine

150 ml/¼ pint whipping cream

1 tablespoon chopped fresh parsley

1 teaspoon chopped fresh dill or chervil

1 tablespoon lemon juice

salt and freshly ground black pepper

creamy, buttery mashed potatoes, to serve

Carefully remove the red corals, then neatly slice the scallops into 3 pieces horizontally.

Melt 15 g/½ oz of the butter in a medium pan and sauté them gently with the corals for 1 minute, then set aside. In the same pan, fry the bacon until crisp, then remove and chop finely. Cook the scallions (spring onions) and mushrooms in the fat from the bacon, adding the remaining butter, for 2–3 minutes, then sprinkle in the flour, stirring well until the flour is cooked. Stir in the wine and bubble gently, stirring until the sauce thickens, then add the cream, bacon, parsley, dill and a little lemon juice. Check the seasoning and bring back to the boil. Return the scallops and allow to heat through, 1–2 minutes.

Creamy, buttery mashed potatoes are the perfect partner for this rich ragout.

Opposite: Dun Aengus stone fort, Aran Islands, County Galway.
Overleaf: Skellig Michael, Iveragh Peninsula, County Kerry.

BRAISED STUFFED PHEASANTS WITH IRISH WHISKEY SAUCE

SERVES 4–6 (LARGE COCK PHEASANTS WILL SERVE 3 PEOPLE GENEROUSLY, BUT HENS ARE CONSIDERED FINER EATING)

Pheasants are in plentiful supply during the season from October to January and are usually sold prepared and neatly packed at the butcher or supermarket. Braising the birds keeps them moist and tender.

2 pheasants
75 g/3 oz butter
6 celery sticks, roughly chopped
4 carrots, roughly chopped
4 onions, roughly chopped
fresh parsley and thyme sprigs
300 ml/½ pint chicken stock
4 tablespoons redcurrant jelly
a large glass of Irish whiskey
300 ml/½ pint whipping cream
salt and freshly ground black pepper

FOR THE STUFFING

110 g/4 oz hazelnuts
55 g/2 oz butter
1 tablespoon each finely chopped carrot, celery and onion
2 streaky bacon strips, chopped
1 orange
6 tablespoons cooked wild and basmati rice mixture
1 tablespoon Irish whiskey

chestnuts and game chips, to garnish (optional, see Notes)

To make the stuffing, lightly brown the hazelnuts in a heavy pan, rub off any loose skins and chop the nuts finely. In the same pan, melt a knob of butter and sauté the chopped vegetables and bacon. Grate the zest of the orange and mix together with the other ingredients, the rice and remaining butter. Moisten with a tablespoon each of whiskey and orange juice. Season well. When cold, stuff the birds loosely and secure with a cocktail stick. Wrap any surplus stuffing in foil and put in the pot with the birds.

In a heavy casserole that will just fit the two birds, melt 55 g/2 oz of the butter and brown the birds all over. Remove. Put in the chopped vegetables and a few sprigs of parsley and thyme. Lay the birds on top, on their sides, and pour on the stock. Season the birds well. Cover the casserole, sealing it well with foil, if necessary. Cook gently for 20 minutes. Then turn the pheasants and cook for a further 15–20 minutes. Test by inserting a skewer between the leg and the breast. The liquid should be faintly pink; pheasants do not benefit from overcooking. Remove the birds and keep them warm.

Strain off the liquid from the vegetables and remove as much fat as possible. Blend the liquid with the redcurrant jelly and pour into a small saucepan. Add the remaining whiskey, heat for a few moments, and then ignite to burn off the alcohol and concentrate the flavour. Now add the cream, taste for seasoning, and boil hard to reduce by about one-third. Finally, whisk in a little butter. Arrange the birds on a large serving dish, tuck the feathers under the tails, if you have them, and glaze with a little of the sauce. Pheasants are traditionally garnished with chestnuts and game chips, or served on a bed of spinach, finished in butter and garlic.

Notes: to prepare chestnuts, make a cross in the skins with a sharp knife and simmer for 20 minutes; cool and peel. Return to the water and continue cooking until they are tender. Cooked chestnuts can be bought vac-packed or in tins.

Game chips are made by slicing peeled potatoes very thinly into cold water. Remove from the water, dry and fry in hot oil. Drain and sprinkle with salt.

LAMB WITH CRAB APPLE JELLY

SERVES 4–6

Crab apples can often be found for the taking in autumn, in woodland areas and along roadsides. They are abundant in Killarney, and their wild and winey flavour gives character to this simple sauce. Ordinary apple jelly can be enhanced by the addition of a little redcurrant jelly or use Rowanberry Jelly (see page 170).

1–2 racks of lamb (4–6 cutlets each)

3 tablespoons olive oil

a large glass each of red wine and stock

3 large garlic cloves

2–3 fresh rosemary sprigs or 1 teaspoon dried rosemary

2 tablespoons dried pink peppercorns (rose peppers)

3 tablespoons crab-apple jelly

lemon juice, to taste

30 g/1 oz butter, chilled and cubed

sea salt and freshly ground black pepper

fresh rosemary sprigs, to garnish

Trim the lamb of any excess fat and neatly pare the cutlet bones. Season with black pepper and rub over with some of the olive oil. Place in a deep dish and pour the wine and stock over. Crush the garlic cloves and tuck them, with the rosemary, around the meat. Marinate for at least half an hour, or overnight.

When ready to cook, reheat the oven to 220°C/425°F/Gas Mark 7.

Remove the meat from the marinade and blot dry with kitchen paper. In a hot pan, brown the racks briefly in a spoonful of oil. Rub a little more oil over the meat and sprinkle the skin with salt. Roast for 15–16 minutes for pink lamb, and 5 minutes or so longer if you prefer it less pink. Remove the lamb to a dish, cover it with foil and a tea towel and allow it to rest.

Strain the marinade into a saucepan, add a sprig of rosemary and the pink peppercorns (if you can only find the brined sort, rise off the brine and use only 1 tablespoon). Boil rapidly to reduce, then add the crab apple jelly, whisking well to dissolve. Taste, adding a little lemon juice if it's too sweet. Pour any juices from the roasting tin into the sauce, remove the rosemary and whisk in the butter, a piece at a time.

Slice the lamb into cutlets, 2 or 3 per person, depending on size. Pour a small pool of sauce on each plate and arrange the cutlets on top. Garnish with the rosemary sprigs.

ROAST MICHAELMAS GOOSE, WITH PRUNE, APPLE AND POTATO STUFFING

SERVES 6

The tradition of a goose for dinner on the feast of St Michael (29 September) is as old as that of the Christmas goose, and made good sense: geese born in the spring were turned out to fatten among the stubble after the grain was harvested, making them nice and plump for Michaelmas.

4–5.5 kg/10–12 lb goose
1 onion, sliced
25 g/½ oz butter
350 g/12 oz prunes, soaked, stoned and chopped
450 g/1 lb apples, chopped
450 g/1 lb potatoes, cooked and mashed
1 teaspoon caraway seeds
1 tablespoon Dijon mustard
1 tablespoon grated orange rind
1 tablespoon chopped fresh sage or ½ teaspoon dried
1 tablespoon sea salt
freshly ground black pepper
Sautéed Cabbage (see page 106), to serve

To drain some of the fat and dry the skin in readiness for roasting crisply, prick the goose thoroughly all over with a fork. Pour boiling water over the skin and leave to dry in an airy place while you make the stuffing.

Preheat the oven to 425°F/220°C/Gas Mark 7.

Cook the sliced onion in the butter until soft, then mix with the chopped prunes, apples and mashed potato. Add the caraway seeds, mustard, orange rind and herbs and season well. When ready to cook, pack the stuffing loosely into the cavity and put any surplus into a foil-covered dish to cook separately. Secure the legs in place by passing a skewer through the first joint of one leg through to the other leg, or tie securely in place.

Dry the goose skin with kitchen paper and rub well with the sea salt. Sit the goose, breast-side down, on a rack in a deep roasting tin and cook for 40 minutes, turning the goose breast-side up after 20 minutes. Lower the heat to 300°F/150°C/Gas Mark 2. Allow about 20 minutes per 450 g/1 lb and test by inserting a skewer between the leg and the breast; clear liquid indicates that it is done. There will be a great deal of fat, so it is more manageable to pour it off once or twice during cooking. Reserve the fat for roasting potatoes. When the goose is ready, cover it with foil and a towel to rest for at least 30–40 minutes.

To make the gravy, add a little stock (made with the giblets, etc.) and a glass of wine or 2 tablespoons orange juice to the de-fatted sediment in the roasting tin, scraping it up well. Boil to reduce, then whisk in a few knobs of butter or a little cream.

Serve with the Sautéed Cabbage.

Opposite: Killarney Lake, County Kerry.

PORK AND APPLE PIE

SERVES 4 AS A MAIN COURSE OR 8 AS A STARTER

This pie is based on one given by Hannah Glasse in her famous 1758 cookery book, The Art of Cookery Made Plain and Easy. This book circulated so widely in Ireland it was said that in some homes of the day it was the only book!

2 large onions, peeled and finely chopped
30 g/1 oz butter
900 g/2 lb good sausagemeat or equal quantities of pork pieces
    and pork belly, finely minced
110 g/4 oz streaky bacon, chopped finely
675 g/1½ lb eating or cooking apples, such as Cox's
    or Bramleys, chopped
30 g/1 oz brown sugar
2–3 fresh sage leaves, chopped, or a little dried sage
5–6 juniper berries, lightly crushed
a small glass of white wine or cider
salt, freshly ground black pepper and grated nutmeg
1 egg, beaten, to glaze

FOR THE PASTRY
450 g/1 lb plain flour
225 g/8 oz butter
1 egg
1–2 tablespoons very cold water
salt, pinch

Make the pastry in the usual way, adding an egg as well as water, and leave to rest. Line a greased 23 cm/ 9 inch square cake tin with baking parchment. Using two-thirds of the pastry, roll out to line the tin, using the remainder for the lid. Keep the trimmings for decoration.

Preheat the oven to 180°C/350°F/Gas Mark 4.

Sauté the onions in half the butter until soft. Cool and add to the sausagemeat, bacon, apples and sugar. Season well with pepper, a little salt and a good grating of nutmeg. Put in the sage (be sparing if the sage is dried). Spread the meat in the pastry case, pushing the juniper berries down into the mixture. Pour over the wine or cider and dot with the remaining butter. If pork is used, add a little more butter (about 55 g/2 oz). Cover with the pastry lid, dampening and pressing the edges well together, make leaves with the pastry trimmings to decorate and then brush the top with the beaten egg.

Bake for about 1 hour, covering the top with foil if it's getting too brown. When cold, cut into squares and serve with a green salad, fruity chutney and good bread.

Note: this pie improves in flavour if it can be left in the fridge for a day or two before cutting.

CHICKEN PIE WITH CASHEW NUTS

SERVES 4–6

This chicken pie is ideal comfort food for cold evenings.
The cashews can be replaced by toasted whole almonds.

1 onion, chopped

3 carrots

1 bay leaf

900 ml/1½ pints water

2 celery sticks

4 large chicken breasts

2 chicken legs

1 tablespoon oil

75 g/3 oz cashew nuts

8 shallots, peeled

2 teaspoons chopped fresh tarragon or a pinch of dried

2 tablespoons plain flour

2 tablespoons butter

salt, freshly ground black pepper and grated nutmeg

FOR THE TOPPING

675 g/1½ lb potatoes

30 g/1 oz butter

hot milk

Put the onion, 1 carrot and the bay leaf in the water and cook for 40 minutes, to make a stock. Remove the carrot and bay leaf from the stock. Cut the remaining carrots and the celery into thick slices and add, with the chicken, to the stock. Cook until the vegetables are cooked but still crisp, then remove with a slotted spoon. Remove the breasts as soon as they are just cooked, after 12–15 minutes, and continue cooking the legs until they are tender.

Skin and bone the chicken legs and put the meat with the breasts. Cut the meat into neat pieces. Return the trimmings to the stock and boil hard to reduce to about 600 ml/1 pint. Preheat the oven to 200°C/400°F/Gas Mark 6.

In a small pan, heat a teaspoon of oil and toast the nuts for a few moments; remove the nuts and cook the shallots in the same pan until they are nicely browned. Add a ladleful of stock and continue to cook until they are tender. Arrange the nuts, vegetables and the chicken pieces in a pie dish and season well. Add a little chopped fresh tarragon, less if using dried.

Cook the flour in the melted butter in a large saucepan and then gradually add the strained hot stock, stirring well until the sauce thickens. Season well with salt, pepper and nutmeg and pour over the chicken and vegetables in the pie dish.

Boil the potatoes in their skins until tender, then drain, peel and mash vigorously – be generous with the butter – fluff up with a fork and add just enough hot milk to make them creamy. Spread over the chicken and cook in the top of the oven until the sauce is bubbling and the potatoes are golden brown.

BAKED COD WITH MUSHROOMS

SERVES 4–6

1 medium onion
1 leek
55 g/2 oz butter
4–6 cod cutlets or fillets
225 g/8 oz mushrooms, sliced
grated zest of ½ lemon
1 dessertspoon plain flour
300 ml/½ pint hot fish stock or milk
6 anchovy fillets, split in half (optional)
30 g/1 oz breadcrumbs
salt and freshly ground black pepper
chopped fresh parsley, to garnish

Below: Cloghane in winter.

Preheat the oven to 170°C/325°F/Gas Mark 3.

Chop the onion finely and slice the cleaned leek. Cook them gently in half the butter until soft. Spread in a buttered ovenproof dish and place the seasoned fish on top.

In the same pan, melt the remaining butter and cook the sliced mushrooms and lemon zest for several minutes until the juices have run and the mushrooms are beginning to brown. Add the flour and stir well until the flour is cooked, about 2–3 minutes. Gradually add the stock or milk, stirring well to prevent lumps from forming. Pour the sauce over the fish and leek mixture. If you are using anchovies, arrange them on top of the sauce. Sprinkle the breadcrumbs over the top. Bake for 25 minutes. Serve sprinkled with parsley.

RABBIT WITH ALMONDS

SERVES 4

Rabbit, enjoying a great revival, was immensely popular in the past. Dozens of recipes survive from Irish household recipe books. Almonds, too, were widely used for flavour and texture in a variety of dishes. Today's tender rabbits are specially bred for the table. Wild rabbits take rather longer to cook and have a gamier flavour.

1.15–1.3 kg/2½–3 lb rabbit, cut into 8–10 pieces
1 tablespoon vinegar
1 tablespoon salt
175 g/6 oz blanched whole almonds
2 tablespoons plain flour
30 g/1 oz butter
1 tablespoon oil
2 onions, sliced
110 g/4 oz streaky bacon, chopped
2 tablespoons Irish whiskey
a fresh thyme sprig
1 bay leaf
a glass of white wine
a glass of stock or water
grated zest and juice of 1 lemon
salt and freshly ground black pepper
plain boiled rice, to serve

Soak the rabbit pieces for 1 hour in water, with the vinegar and salt. If the rabbit is wild, soak overnight. In a large frying pan, lightly brown the almonds with a teaspoon of oil.

Preheat the oven to 180°C/350°F/Gas Mark 4.

Remove the rabbit pieces from the water, rinse well and pat dry. Season the pieces and flour well. Brown the rabbit in the butter and oil in an ovenproof casserole. Add the onions and bacon and continue cooking until softened slightly. Add the whiskey, the herbs, wine, stock or water, lemon juice and zest, and the almonds. Check the seasoning.

Cover tightly and transfer to the oven and cook for about 1 hour. Test with a skewer and add a little more wine or stock if it needs more cooking or seems to be dry.

Serve the rabbit and almonds arranged on a dish of plain boiled rice and pour the pan juices on top.

Opposite: Wild flower meadow.

RAGOUT OF COD AND CLAMS

SERVES 6

In the past, clams made only very occasional appearances on our western shores, but in recent years they have been cultivated very successfully and have found a natural place in Irish cooking. Basmati rice or new potatoes, buttered and sprinkled with herbs, are good served with this.

2 large onions
1 tablespoon olive oil
2 garlic cloves
3 tablespoons balsamic vinegar
300 ml/½ pint fish or chicken stock
2 x 400 g/14 oz tins chopped Italian tomatoes
1 tablespoon chopped fresh coriander
675 g/1½ lb cod
675 g/1½ lb clams, scrubbed
salt and freshly ground black pepper
basmati rice or new potatoes with
    butter and herbs, to serve

Slice the onions into fine rings and put them in a heavy, flameproof casserole or saucepan, with the oil and garlic. Sauté gently until they are soft but not brown, then add the balsamic vinegar and the stock. Cover and cook over a moderate heat until the stock has almost evaporated and become slightly syrupy, but watch that it doesn't burn. This takes about 10–15 minutes.

Now add the tomatoes and coriander and cook for a further 10 minutes to reduce slightly. Taste for seasoning. Cut the cod in large cubes and add, with the clams, still in their shells, to the sauce. Cover and cook gently for 6–7 minutes until the cod is cooked and the clams have opened. Discard any clams that are still closed. Add a few grinds of black pepper and serve with rice or buttered potatoes.

SPICED BEEF

Spiced beef is one of the seasonal pleasures of Christmas. Decorated with holly and embalmed in spice, it can be seen in every butcher's shop during the Christmas season. To make it at home, you must start a week or ten days before it is required.

4½ lb/2kg beef brisket

FOR THE PICKLE

225 g/8 oz salt
1 tablespoon saltpetre (see Notes)
110 g/4 oz brown sugar
300 ml/½ pint Guinness

FOR THE SPICE MIX

2 teaspoons each ground black pepper, grated nutmeg, fresh thyme, ground mace
1 teaspoon ground clove
3 teaspoons allspice
2 bay leaves, crushed
1 onion, finely chopped

In a good sized saucepan put the salt, saltpetre, brown sugar and Guinness. Add 1.5 litres cold water, then bring slowly to the boil and simmer for 10 minutes. Turn off the heat and allow to cool. Cover the meat with the cold brine and transfer to the fridge for 7 days (or 10 days if you are making Corned Beef), turning the meat in the pickle every day.

Remove the meat from the pickle, drain and dry. (Discard the pickle.) Mix the spices and onions together and rub thoroughly into the meat. Reserve the surplus spices. Wrap the meat in cling film and return to the fridge for a further 3–4 days, turning and rubbing in more spice each day. Top up the spices as necessary.

Finally, return the meat to a clean saucepan, cover with cold water, bring to the boil slowly and simmer gently for 3–3½ hours, checking with a skewer after 2¾ hours. Cool in the liquid before drying and wrapping in foil. Keep in the fridge for a week to 10 days. Any remaining spice can be rubbed into the meat before wrapping in foil.

This sounds like a lot of work, but in fact it doesn't really take a lot of time once the ingredients are assembled. Remembering to attend to it each day is the difficult part.

Serve the beef cold, cut in fine slices on a bed of rocket with Dijon mustard, a good fruity chutney or cranberry sauce on the side. It can also be eaten hot, rather like ham.

Notes: the final cooking can be done in the oven if preferred. Bring to the boil as above, then transfer to the oven at 180°C/350°F/ Gas Mark 4, checking as above.

Saltpetre is not essential, rather it is used to preserve the colour of the meat. It is available on the internet or you can use Prague Powder Number 1 (also known as 'pink salts') which can be bought from your butcher.

VENISON PASTIES

These small pasties are a manageable version of the great decorated venison pies of the past. These were 'side board' dishes which allowed the pastry cooks to show off their art. Widely available during the winter, both farmed and wild, venison is a lean meat and benefits from being marinated before cooking for as long as time allows.

900 g/2 lb breast of venison, or pieces

2 tablespoons olive oil

2 tablespoons red-wine vinegar

2 garlic cloves, crushed

1 teaspoon ground mace

6–7 juniper berries, slightly crushed

2 large onions

1 carrot

1 celery stick

110 g/4 oz piece of fat bacon

900 g/2 lb puff pastry

1 egg, beaten

salt and freshly ground black pepper

Cut the venison into cubes and put them in an ovenproof dish, with the oil, vinegar, crushed garlic, mace and juniper berries. Leave overnight, if possible.

Preheat the oven to 160°C/325°F/Gas Mark 3. Chop the vegetables finely. Cut the bacon into small cubes and fry until crisp. Add the bacon and vegetables to the meat and marinade, cover and bake for 45 minutes to 1 hour, or until the meat is just tender, but check once or twice because venison doesn't benefit from overcooking. Remove and cool.

Turn the oven up to 180°C/350°F/Gas Mark 4.

Roll out the pastry out to make 6 pieces 15 x 20 cm/6 x 8 inches, patching together if necessary. Pour off and keep any excess gravy from the meat filling. Divide the filling among the pastry pieces, putting it in the centre and leaving a gap of 5 cm/2 inches on either side and 2.5 cm/1 inch at the top and bottom. Dampen the edges with beaten egg and draw the sides together, pinching well. Pinch together the tops and bottoms securely. Line a baking tray with baking parchment and lay the pasties on it, seam-side down, and make a hole in the top. Brush over with beaten egg, decorate as lavishly as the pastry trimmings will allow.

Bake for about 40–45 minutes until the pastry is golden brown. The remaining gravy can be handed round separately, with a dash of lemon juice added. Redcurrant or Rowanberry Jelly (see page 170) is very good with venison.

BEEF AND MUSHROOM PIE WITH GUINNESS

SERVES 6

Leg or shin of beef is a great choice for slow cooking, for, although it takes a long time to cook initially, it remains tender and juicy.

900 g/2 lb leg or shin of beef, trimmed and cubed

2 tablespoons plain flour

2 tablespoons olive oil

1 bay leaf

1 fresh thyme spring

1 fresh parsley or sage sprig

2 large onions, chopped

1 carrot, chopped

1 celery stick, chopped

4 tinned anchovies, drained

450 ml/¾ pint Guinness

225 g/8 oz mushrooms

225 g/8 oz puff pastry

1 egg, beaten

salt and freshly ground black pepper

mashed or baby new potatoes, or crusty
   bread and salad, to serve

Toss the beef in the flour and brown in the oil in a large saucepan. Tie the bay leaf, thyme and parsley to make a bouquet garni. Add the onions to the pan and toss until they begin to soften then add the carrot, celery, the bouquet garni and seasoning. Mash the anchovies and stir in. Pour the Guinness over the top, stir well, cover and cook very gently until the meat is almost tender, about 1½ hours. (This can be done in the oven if preferred, at 180°C/350°F/Gas Mark 4.) Add the mushrooms and continue cooking for another 25 minutes. Allow the filling to cool.

Preheat the oven to 190°C/375°F/Gas Mark 5.

Transfer the contents of the saucepan to a deep pie dish and check the seasoning. Roll the pastry out on a floured board into a large circle about 4 cm/1½ inches larger than the pie dish. Cut the surplus off in a long strip and press on to the dampened edge of the dish. Lay the remaining pastry circle over the pie, pressing on to the strip to attach it well and crimping the edges decoratively. Make a vent in the centre and decorate the pie with leaves or flowers made from the pastry trimmings. Brush with the beaten egg and bake for 45–50 minutes until the pastry is risen and golden.

Eat this with creamy mashed potatoes or baby new potatoes tossed in butter and parsley or fresh crusty bread and a green salad.

BREAST OF CHICKEN WITH WALNUT AND APPLE

SERVES 4

'On rainy days alone I dine,
Upon a chick, and pint of wine.
On rainy days I dine alone,
And pick my chicken to the bone.'

Jonathan Swift

55 g/2 oz butter
½ large Bramley cooking apple, peeled and chopped
4 fresh sage leaves, finely chopped, or a tiny pinch of dried sage
75 g/3 oz walnuts, chopped
4 large chicken breasts
2 tablespoons plain flour
1 egg, beaten
75 g/3 oz breadcrumbs
1 tablespoon oil
150 ml/¼ pint double cream
½ teaspoon paprika
salt and freshly ground black pepper

In a small pan, melt 15 g/½ oz of the butter and add the apple, sage and walnuts. Cook gently until the apple is just beginning to soften and the walnuts beginning to colour. Set aside to cool and season well.

Make a long, deep incision in the sides of the chicken breasts, cutting lengthways to make a deep pocket. Divide the stuffing among the chicken breasts, pushing it well into the pockets. Season and flour the chicken and then dip the chicken in egg and roll in breadcrumbs. Secure with cocktail sticks. (If the chicken is being prepared in advance, chill the stuffing before inserting it.)

In a large pan, melt 30 g/1 oz of the butter with the oil and fry the chicken gently, turning once or twice, until cooked and golden, but still moist, about 5–7 minutes on each side, depending on thickness. Remove the chicken and keep warm. Wipe any burnt crumbs from the pan with kitchen paper and pour in the cream. Add any remaining stuffing or crumbs, season well with salt, pepper and paprika and bubble up for a few moments, scraping up the sediment; whisk in the remaining butter and pour over the chicken.

Opposite: Cliffs of Moher, County Clare.

STUFFED PORK CHOPS WITH POTATO-APPLE FRITTERS

SERVES 4

4 loin chops, 2.5 cm/1 inch thick
1 tablespoon balsamic vinegar
grated zest and juice of 1 lemon
1 tablespoon Dijon mustard
chopped fresh parsley
55 g/2 oz brown breadcrumbs
finely chopped fresh thyme
40 g/1½ oz butter
1 tablespoon grated fresh root ginger
1 eating apple, Cox's pippin or similar, peeled and finely chopped
1 egg, beaten
1 tablespoon oil
150 ml/¼ pint cider, white wine or chicken stock
salt and freshly ground black pepper

FOR THE FRITTERS

225 g/8 oz raw potato, grated
110 g/4 oz apple, grated
55 g/2 oz plain flour
2 eggs
2 tablespoons whipping cream
oil and butter, for frying
salt

Make cuts in the fat along the edge of the chops at 1 cm/½ inch intervals (this helps the fat to cook and prevents the chops from curling up when heated). Make a horizontal incision in the side of each chop, to form a pocket. Mix the vinegar, lemon juice and mustard together and toss the meat well in this mixture. Leave to marinate while you make the stuffing, or longer, if time allows.

Put the parsley in a bowl with the lemon zest, breadcrumbs and thyme. Melt 15 g/½ oz of the butter in a large pan and cook the ginger for a few moments, then add the apple and cook until soft. Mix in the breadcrumbs, season well and bind with the beaten egg. Allow to cool.

Spoon the stuffing into the pockets in the chops and secure with cocktail sticks or poultry pins. Add half the remaining butter and the oil to the pan, turn up the heat and brown the chops well on either side. Add the cider, wine or stock and the remaining marinade. Cover the pan, lower the heat and cook very gently until the chops are done – 6–8 minutes, turning once or twice. Remove the chops to a serving dish and keep warm.

Add the remaining butter to the pan, scrape up the residue, bubble for a few moments to reduce, check and adjust the seasoning, and pour over the chops. Keep the chops warm while you make the fritters.

Mix the potato and apples together with the flour. Bind with the eggs and cream and mix to a batter consistency. Fry, a tablespoon at a time, in hot oil and butter for 3–5 minutes until crisp and golden brown; drain on kitchen paper and sprinkle with salt before serving with the chops.

ROAST TURKEY WITH STUFFING

SERVES 8–10

This tturkey has two stuffings and is semi-braised, to retain moisture.

5.5 kg/1 lb turkey
55 g/2 oz butter
2 large onions, halved
8 cloves
2 carrots, coarsely chopped
2 celery sticks, coarsely chopped
225 g/8 oz bacon, cut into strips
300 ml/½ pint cider or white wine
salt and freshly ground black pepper

FOR THE PRUNE AND CHICKEN LIVER STUFFING

1 large onion, finely chopped
55 g/2 oz butter
225 g/8 oz chicken livers, cleaned and chopped
350 g/12 oz fresh breadcrumbs
1 celery stick, finely chopped
1 carrot, grated
225 g/8 oz prunes, stoned and chopped
a small glass of vermouth or sherry
2 teaspoons dried mixed herbs
1 teaspoon ground mace
salt and freshly ground black pepper

FOR THE APPLE AND WALNUT STUFFING

175 g/6 oz walnuts, chopped
2 cooking apples, peeled and chopped
55 g/2 oz butter, softened
1 tablespoon grated fresh root ginger
55 g/2 oz fresh breadcrumbs
salt and freshly ground black pepper

Opposite: A peaceful night in County Sligo.

Preheat the oven to 230°C/450°F/Gas Mark 8.

To make the prune stuffing, cook the onion in half the butter, then add the livers and cook until slightly pink. Add to the breadcrumbs. In the remaining butter, cook the celery, carrot and prunes for a few minutes, then add the vermouth or sherry, herbs, mace and seasoning. Bubble up well. Mix into the breadcrumbs and cool.

To make the apple stuffing, mix all the ingredients together and season well. Stuff the turkey's body cavity loosely with the prune stuffing. Insert slices of butter under the breast skin. Skewer or tie the legs together. Stuff the crop with the apple stuffing and secure with a skewer. Season the turkey thoroughly and rub the breast well with butter. Put the halved onions, stuck with the cloves, in a deep roasting pan with the vegetables, bacon and cider. Lay the turkey on its side on top.

Put the turkey in the oven and immediately lower the heat to 180°C/350°F/Gas Mark 4. After 45 minutes, turn the turkey on to the other side and baste well. After a further 45 minutes, turn the turkey breast-side up and continue cooking for a further 45 minutes to an hour, basting well and covering the breast with foil if it is browning too fast. Test by inserting a skewer between the thigh and the breast; the juices should be clear. Remove the turkey to a dish and cover with foil and a towel; leave the meat to relax to keep it juicy and allow the juices to be reabsorbed. It will stay warm for 45 minutes to 1 hour.

To make the gravy, strain off the stock from the roasting tin and leave it to stand so the fat rises to the top. Remove the fat and set it aside. Mix 1 tablespoon of flour with 1 tablespoon of the fat in a saucepan, stir well, cooking for 2 minutes, then blend in the stock. Boil hard to thicken slightly and reduce. Pour into a sauceboat and serve very hot. Crisp bacon rolls and mini sausages can be used to garnish the dish and cranberry or Rowanberry Jelly (see page 170) can be handed round separately.

SALADS AND SIDES

SALAD OF LAMB'S LETTUCE AND DANDELION LEAVES

SERVES 6

Dandelions are thought to have great curative powers: true or not, I couldn't say; but they make a great salad.

225 g/8 oz lamb's lettuce
225 g/8 oz young dandelion leaves
3 tablespoons wine or cider vinegar
6 rindless streaky bacon rashers
1 garlic clove
55–75 g/2–3 oz Cashel Blue cheese
salt and freshly ground black pepper

FOR THE VINAIGRETTE
1 teaspoon French mustard
1 tablespoon cider or wine vinegar
4–5 tablespoons olive oil
salt and freshly ground black pepper

Wash the lamb's lettuce and set aside to drain. Wash the dandelion leaves and trim the stalks. Dry well, then put them in the salad bowl. Heat the vinegar and pour it over the dandelion leaves; toss and leave for about 15 minutes. This helps to soften them. Pour off any surplus vinegar.

Meanwhile, make the vinaigrette, mixing the mustard, vinegar and salt and pepper together and whisking in the oil until smooth.

Fry the bacon in its own fat, with the garlic, until crisp. Remove the garlic and pour the bacon and pan juices over the dandelions. Add the lamb's lettuce to the bowl and toss well with a little of the vinaigrette. Season to taste. Crumble the cheese on top and serve while the bacon is still warm.

Above right: Brandon Mountain, Dingle Peninsula, County Kerry.
Previous page: An old fishing boat on Lough Gill.

CHICKEN, ORANGE AND ROCKET SALAD WITH WALNUT SAUCE

SERVES 6

Large boneless, skinless chicken breasts,
    weighing about 450 g/1 lb in total
300 ml/½ pint chicken stock
18–20 rocket leaves
2 large sweet oranges, or 3 small ones
salt

FOR THE SAUCE

90 g/3½ oz walnut halves
1 tablespoon cider or sherry vinegar
3 tablespoons walnut or olive oil
2 teaspoons sugar
1 garlic clove

Put the chicken in a saucepan and barely cover with the stock. Add a pinch of salt and poach gently until cooked but still moist, about 10–15 minutes. Remove the chicken to cool. Reserve the stock and strain. Shred the chicken by pulling it apart with 2 forks, lengthways, with the grain of the meat.

Wash and dry the rocket leaves and put in the fridge to crisp.

To make the sauce, toast the walnuts in a dry pan until crisp and just beginning to brown. Put them in a blender with the other sauce ingredients and half the reserved stock. Grind to a smooth paste. Taste, adding more vinegar or sugar as you like. Use the remaining stock to dilute the sauce to the desired texture. Reserve 2 tablespoons of the sauce to finish.

Peel the oranges with a sharp knife, then slice down between the segments and separate the flesh from the dividing membrane. Allow 2 or 3 segments per person. All of this can be prepared ahead of time, or the day before.

To serve, pour a small pool of sauce on each plate and arrange some of the chicken, topped with orange and rocket, on each. Thin the remaining 2 tablespoons of sauce with more stock or oil and drizzle over the top.

Opposite: Kells Bay Gardens in County Kerry.

PEAS AND LETTUCE

SERVES 6

This combination of two summer vegetables is more than 200 years old and, though its origins are French, it pops up frequently in old Irish recipe collections. No need to wait for summer: the frozen petit pois available in the chill cabinet are a great substitute for the tender young summer peas. Equally delicious with fish, chicken or lamb.

450 g/1 lb petits pois, thawed, or small fresh peas
4 baby gem lettuce
30 g/1 oz butter
3–4 scallions (spring onions), finely chopped
150 ml/¼ pint whipping cream
2 tablespoons chopped fresh chervil or basil
salt and freshly ground black pepper

Defrost the peas by pouring boiling water over them. Drain well. Wash the lettuce and remove any damaged leaves. Cut each into eighths lengthways.

Melt the butter in a large frying pan or saucepan and gently cook the scallions (spring onions). Add the peas, lettuce, cream, herbs and seasonings. Cover for 5 minutes or so to soften the lettuce, but don't allow it to break up. Remove the lid and check the seasoning. Simmer gently for 8 minutes before serving.

ROAST BEEF SALAD

SERVES 6–8

A fillet of Irish beef needs few extras and is at its best simply prepared. For this summery salad, both beef and sauce can be prepared well in advance.

FOR THE BEEF

675 g/1½ lb beef fillet, in one piece, trimmed and tied

4 tablespoons olive oil, plus extra for blending

2 tablespoons red wine vinegar

2 garlic cloves, crushed

2 teaspoons ground allspice

1 tablespoon Dijon mustard

FOR THE SALAD

2 bunches of scallions (spring onions)

mixed lettuce and herb leaves

cherry tomatoes

marigold petals, chive or rocket flowers

FOR THE SAUCE

2 tablespoons white wine vinegar

1 teaspoon peppercorns

2 teaspoons each chopped fresh tarragon and parsley, mixed

4 tablespoons water

4 egg yolks

175 g/6 oz unsalted butter, softened

Trim the meat of any fat and tie it around at intervals to keep its shape while cooking. Marinate the meat at room temperature in the oil, vinegar and crushed garlic for 2–3 hours.

Preheat the oven to 220°C/425°F/Gas Mark 7.

Remove the beef from the marinade and wipe dry with kitchen paper. Mix the allspice and mustard into a paste with a little oil and spread over the meat. Roast the meat for 20 minutes. This will give pink beef. Cook for 5–7 minutes longer if preferred.

Five minutes before the end of the cooking time, brush the scallions (spring onions) with olive oil and scatter over the meat. Remove the meat to a cool place to prevent further cooking.

To make the sauce, boil the vinegar, peppercorns and 1 teaspoon of the herbs with the water until reduced to about 2 tablespoons. Strain into a bowl over hot water, or use a double-boiler, and beat in the egg yolks. Stir well until the yolks are warm, then gradually stir in the softened butter, in walnut-sized lumps, stirring until the sauce thickens slightly and will coat the back of a spoon. Stir continuously, lifting the saucepan on and off the heat to prevent it from overheating and scrambling the eggs. When the sauce has thickened, pour it into a blender and whizz for a few moments until it becomes slightly foamy. Alternatively, whisk hard with a wire whisk. Then add the remaining herbs, cover and set aside. Pour into a serving dish.

Arrange the lettuce and other leaves on a large serving dish. Untie the beef and slice very thinly. Arrange in an overlapping circle and put the leaves and wilted scallions (spring onions) in the centre. Garnish with the tomatoes and whatever herb flowers are to hand – marigold petals, chive or rocket flowers. Spoon a little vinaigrette over the leaves just before serving. Serve extra sauce separately.

Note: the beef will lose its pink colour and darken if sliced too soon.

SAUTÉED CABBAGE
WITH BACON

SERVES 4

225 g/8 oz piece streaky bacon, cubed

2 tablespoons oil

2 tablespoons wine vinegar

6 tablespoons water

1 teaspoon sugar

1 teaspoon caraway seeds

550 g/1¼ lb finely sliced or shredded cabbage,
    hard stalks removed

1 large Bramley cooking apple, peeled and chopped

salt and freshly ground black pepper

Cook the bacon cubes in the oil in a large pan until crisp.
Remove and keep warm. Pour off the fat from pan before adding
the vinegar, water, sugar and caraway seeds, scraping up the
sediment, and boiling for a few moments.

Add the cabbage and apple to the pan and cook, turning
frequently until the cabbage is just tender and the apple soft
and melting, about 7–8 minutes. Taste for seasoning, sprinkle
the bacon on top and serve.

This dish is the perfect partner for fowl and game.

Opposite: Fishing in Lough Gill.

COLCANNON

Though variations of Colcannon are eaten all year round, it is an essential part of the Halloween feast, when rings or coins, wrapped in paper, bring marriage or riches to the lucky finders during the coming year.

450 g/1 lb kale or green cabbage
675 g/1½ lb potatoes, unpeeled
1 bunch scallions (spring onions), finely chopped
175 ml/6 fl oz hot cream or milk
110 g/4 oz butter
salt and white pepper

Remove the hard stalks from the kale or cabbage, and cook in salted, boiling water until tender. Kale takes a surprisingly long time, about 25 minutes; cabbage will take 8–10 minutes. Drain, press out any remaining water and chop finely, or use a food processor.

Boil the potatoes in salted boiling water until soft. Peel and mash carefully by hand, removing any lumps, but don't use the food processor – the potatoes turn into glue.

The scallions (spring onions) can be cooked in the cream or milk for a few minutes, though personally I prefer them raw. Add them to the potatoes, with the hot cream or milk, half the butter and the kale or cabbage. Beat thoroughly together, adjust the seasoning, then turn into a large serving bowl. Make a well in the centre, and drop in the remaining butter in one piece, then serve very hot.

COLCANNON – WEXFORD STYLE

SERVES 4

Almost every region of Ireland has its take on colcannon and each claims theirs as the 'true' recipe. Like traditional dishes worldwide, the local version contains whatever is readily available. Wexford's comfortable farms are known for their vegetable gardens and orchards.

8 large potatoes
1 large parsnip
1 large onion
1 cabbage or kale
a bunch of fresh parsley, chopped
110 g/4 oz butter
hot milk
salt and freshly ground black pepper
chopped fresh parsley or chopped scallions (spring onions), to garnish

Peel the potatoes and cook in the usual way until soft. Wash, dry and chop all the vegetables in small pieces, keeping one large cabbage or kale leaf aside. Place them in a steamer or colander over boiling water. Cover with the cabbage leaf and the lid and steam for 30–35 minutes for cabbage or up to 1 hour for kale, until all the vegetables are tender.

Mash the potatoes, vegetables and parsley together. Season with salt and pepper and add 75 g/3 oz of the butter and sufficient hot milk to make it creamy. Serve in a mound on a deep dish with the remaining butter pressed into the centre and chopped parsley or scallions (spring onions) scattered over the top.

Opposite: Trees at the edge of Lough Gill.

GRATIN OF PARSNIPS AND PEARS

SERVES 6

'Fair words butter no parsnips'
Old saying

This is a simple and delicious way with parsnips, which can be prepared a day in advance, popped in the fridge and finished when ready to cook. Excellent with roasts of all sorts and particularly good with golden sausages.

3–4 large parsnips
3 large pears
1 tablespoon lemon juice
55 g/2 oz butter
30 g/1 oz stale breadcrumbs, tossed in a knob of melted butter
grated nutmeg
salt and freshly ground black pepper

Preheat the oven to 180°C/350°F/Gas Mark 4.

Cut the parsnips in quarters lengthways and cut away some of the hard core, then peel, trim and cut into chunks. Peel and core the pears and chop roughly. Put the parsnips and pears in a large saucepan. Add a little salt and the lemon juice and just barely cover with water. Simmer gently until tender. Drain well and mash thoroughly with the butter until smooth and creamy, adding black pepper to taste and a good grating of nutmeg.

Transfer to an oven dish and sprinkle the breadcrumbs over the top. Bake for 15–20 minutes, or until golden brown.

ORANGE, CELERY AND WATERCRESS SALAD

SERVES 6

This winter salad is the classic partner for wild duck, but just as good with tame fowl or pork. Lamb's lettuce or rocket can be used instead of the watercress.

2–3 oranges
1–2 bunches of watercress
6–8 celery sticks, finely sliced
1 small onion, finely chopped
2 tablespoons olive oil
1 tablespoon lemon juice
salt and paprika

Peel the oranges, removing as much pith as possible. Wash and gently shake the watercress dry. Arrange on a flat dish with the celery. Slice the oranges across thinly and arrange on top, removing any pips. Sprinkle the finely chopped onion over the oranges and season with salt.

Dress the salad with oil and lemon just before serving and sprinkle a little paprika over the top.

Below: Calm reflections in Caragh Lake.

DESSERTS

ORANGE CREAMS

SERVES 4

Seville oranges, both zest and pith, were used to make these delicious creams in the past, when oranges were a seasonal commodity. One Seville orange, with its stronger flavour, would be sufficient.

2 oranges
4 egg yolks
2 egg whites
150 ml/¼ pint whipping cream
150 ml/¼ milk
about 2 tablespoons caster sugar
1 tablespoon brandy, rum or orange liqueur
whipped cream, to serve

Choose unwaxed oranges, if possible. Scrub the skins well and then with a potato peeler, peel the zest off, not too thinly (a very little pith will give more flavour). Squeeze the juice. Put the orange zest, juice and 1 tablespoon water into a small saucepan and simmer very gently until the zest is soft. This takes a surprisingly long time, perhaps 45 minutes, and you will probably need to add a few spoonfuls more water from time to time. When the zest is soft, allow the liquid to evaporate, being careful it doesn't burn.

Preheat the oven to 150°C/300°F/Gas Mark 2.

Purée the zest in a mini processor or a mortar and pestle. Add the eggs, cream and milk, sugar to taste and the brandy, rum or liqueur and pour into 4 buttered ramekins. A strip of peel or a small, skinned orange section can be gently laid on top of each.

Set the ramekins in water in a roasting tin and bake for about 35–40 minutes until set when tested with a knife. Serve cold, in the ramekins, with a spoonful of whipped cream on top.

Above and previous page: Coumeenoole Sands and Slea Head, Dingle Peninsula.

CINNAMON CUSTARD

This is delicious with pancakes and it also makes a wonderful filling for a sponge cake.

4 egg yolks
110 g/4 oz caster sugar
55 g/2 oz cornflour
500 ml/17 fl oz milk
½ cinnamon stick
1 vanilla pod
1 teaspoon grated lemon zest

Mix the egg yolks with the sugar and cornflour. Bring the milk to the boil slowly, with the cinnamon stick, vanilla pod and lemon zest, then turn off the heat and leave to infuse for 15 minutes.

Remove the cinnamon and vanilla. Bring the milk back to the boil and pour on to the egg mixture, stirring rapidly. Return the mixture to the saucepan over a low heat, and stir continuously until the mixture thickens slightly. Do not allow to boil, or the eggs will scramble. Pour into a shallow bowl to cool.

To serve, spread the pancakes with a few spoonfuls of the custard, sprinkle with a few drops of brandy and roll up. Reheat in a moderate oven (180°C/350°F/Gas Mark 4), for 15 minutes.

PANCAKES

SERVES 4

These are traditionally eaten on Shrove Tuesday, the day before Lent begins. Shrove Tuesday pancakes are served in the simplest manner, with sugar, lemon juice and butter and it's hard to improve on this. However, for a simple and delicious dessert, fill them with Cinnamon Custard (see left).

225 g/8 oz plain flour
1 tablespoon caster sugar
a pinch of ground ginger or grated nutmeg
2 eggs, beaten
55 g/2 oz butter, melted
600 ml/1 pint milk
oil and melted butter, for frying
custard and seasonal fruits, to serve (optional)

Mix the dry ingredients together and then add the eggs, butter and milk. Beat thoroughly and leave for at least an hour for the flour to expand.

Heat a heavy 18 cm/7 inch frying pan until hot and add a teaspoon each of oil and butter. Swirl around the pan and pour the surplus into a little dish. Pour a small ladleful of batter into the pan and swirl around to form a thin skin. Cook until golden brown, then turn with a palette knife and cook for a few moments longer. (The first couple of pancakes invariably break up or stick.) Dip a pastry brush in oil and melted butter and brush the pan again before cooking each pancake. Stack, with greaseproof paper between each pancake. They can be reheated gently in the oven or microwave. Serve with custard and seasonal fruits, if you like.

Note: don't use a nylon pastry brush – it will melt. A twist of kitchen paper works well.

STRAWBERRIES IN CLARET JELLY

SERVES 6

Eating strawberries with red wine is a very old custom, the acidity of both being tempered by the liberal use of sugar and spice. Choose a wine you would like to drink and think of the poet Keats:

> *'How I like Claret! When I can get Claret, I must drink it….*
> *If you could make some wine like Claret to drink on summer*
> *evenings in an arbour …'*
>
> *John Keats, letter to his brother, 1819*

350 g/12 oz strawberries
600 ml/1 pint claret or other red wine
8 teaspoons/2 x 11 g/½ oz sachets/6 leaves gelatine
200 g/7 oz redcurrant jelly
110 g/4 oz caster sugar, or to taste
1 cinnamon stick
2–3 tablespoons water
2 tablespoons brandy
2 tablespoons lemon juice
strawberries and fruits, to decorate
whipped cream infused with scented
    geranium leaves, to serve

Wipe the strawberries with kitchen paper, and hull them. Put 100 ml of the wine in a small bowl and sprinkle the gelatine over it. When the gelatine has softened, stand the bowl in hot water and stir until the gelatine has completely dissolved. Keep warm.

Heat the redcurrant jelly, sugar and cinnamon stick in a saucepan with the water until both sugar and jelly have dissolved. Taste, you may like more sugar. Remove the cinnamon and strain into a large bowl. Add the gelatine and mix thoroughly, making sure there are no little undissolved globules of gelatine. When cool add the rest of the claret, along with the brandy and lemon juice.

Pour half the mixture and half the strawberries into a dampened 1.2 litre/2 pint jelly mould and allow to set. Warm the remaining jelly mixture, add the rest of the strawberries and fill up the mould. (If this operation is done all at once, the strawberries will float to the top.) Turn out when completely set and decorate with fruits, flowers and leaves.

Have a bowl of whipped cream on hand, for those who like it. A couple of scented geranium leaves, infused in the cream for an hour or so, give a subtle flavour.

Opposite: Upper Lake, Count Kerry.

CHERRY MOUSSE

SERVES 6

450 g/1 lb cherries
1 tablespoon each grated lemon zest and lemon juice
4 teaspoons/11 g/½ oz sachet/3 leaves gelatine
4 eggs
55 g/2 oz caster sugar
150 ml/¼ pint whipping cream
summer fruits or fresh mint leaves, to decorate

Poach the cherries in as little water as possible until soft enough to extract the stones, then drain, reserving any cooking liquid. Purée the cherries with 1–2 tablespoons of the cooking water and the zest and juice of the lemons. Use the remaining cooking water to dissolve the gelatine, topping it up with water according to the directions on the packet.

Separate the eggs and put the yolks and sugar in a bowl over hot water. Whisk, over a low heat until thick and creamy. Remove from the heat and whisk from time to time until cool. Cool the gelatine and stir thoroughly into the egg mixture, then beat in the cherry purée. Lightly whip the cream and fold it in.

Whisk the egg whites to the soft-peak stage and, when the gelatine mixture is on the point of setting, fold the whites in carefully, amalgamating them thoroughly. Divide the mousse among 6 ring moulds or ramekins and allow to set. Decorate with berries or mint leaves.

ROSE-PETAL ICE CREAM

Scented roses are one of the great pleasures of summer. Make the most of them with this romantic ice cream. You can buy rose-water at oriental stores, delicatessens and major supermarkets.

600 ml/1 pint red or pink scented rose petals
110 g/4 oz caster sugar
150 ml/¼ pint rosé wine
5 egg yolks
1 vanilla pod or 1 teaspoon vanilla extract
300 ml/½ pint milk
300 ml/½ pint double cream
½–1 teaspoon rose-water
crystallised rose petals, to decorate (see note)

To prepare the rose petals, wipe them clean with damp kitchen paper and cut away the hard white stem or heel. Put them in a blender or food processor, with 55 g/2 oz sugar and the wine, and purée.

Beat the eggs and remaining sugar thoroughly. Split the vanilla pod, if using, and add to the milk and cream. Bring to the boil and simmer gently for a few moments, to infuse, then remove the pod. Add vanilla extract now, if using. Pour the hot mixture slowly on to the eggs and sugar and return to the saucepan, stirring continuously. Heat to just below boiling point, but don't let it boil. The point is reached when, removing the spoon from the mixture and running the finger along it, the mixture remains separated. Leave to cool.

Mix in the rose purée and rose-water, a drop at a time. Taste for sweetness. Freeze in the usual way, stirring and beating it 2 or 3 times during the freezing process or use an ice cream machine. To serve, decorate with crystallised rose petals.

Note: to make crystallised rose petals, prepare the rose petals as for the ice cream. Beat one large egg white until just fluid. Dip each petal into the egg white and then dredge in caster sugar, covering completely. Cover a baking tray with baking parchment, then spread the petals on it and dry in a very low oven, with the door ajar, for an hour or so until they are crisp. Store in an airtight tin, between sheets of greaseproof paper. They are great for cake decoration, too.

Opposite: Blennerville Village, Tralee.

SYLLABUB

SERVES 4

In the seventeenth century, this was a popular confection of wine, cider or fruit juice to which milk was added by force – often by milking the cow directly into the other ingredients to make froth, or bubbles, hence the name Silly Bubbles. It was also the traditional covering for trifle, before whipped cream became universal.

300 ml/½ pint whipping cream
3 tablespoons sweet white wine or sherry (not dry)
juice of ½ orange
grated zest of ½ lemon
55 g/2 oz caster sugar

TO DECORATE
summer fruits
Macaroons (see page 158)

Whip all the ingredients together until thick and creamy and the mixture will just hold its shape. Carefully spoon into four stemmed glasses. Make the syllabub a few hours in advance to allow the flavours to develop. Garnish with berries and serve with Macaroons.

Left: Waterfall at Kell's Bay Gardens.

AUTUMN PUDDING

SERVES 4–5

This is an autumnal version of summer pudding, a sort of consolation for the passing of the brilliant summer raspberries and redcurrants. In its own way, it's just as nice.

The traditional combination is apples, plums (peeled, stoned and cut into small cubes) and blackberries. The bread should be stale, at least two days old and anything from sliced pan to brioche is suitable, if it can be cut to shape. Left-over Barm Brack (see page 160) is excellent. Homemade custard, hot or cold, or whipped cream mixed with crème fraîche, are equally good on the side.

900 g/2 lb mixed fruit, e.g. apples, plums,
    blackberries and autumn rhubarb
caster sugar to taste (optional)
a little butter, for greasing
8–10 stale bread slices
custard or whipped cream, to serve (optional)

Cook the fruit gently in a saucepan, using as little water as possible to moisten it (1–2 tablespoons at most) or, better still, cook it in the microwave until just soft and the juice is just beginning to run. Sweeten to taste. Strain off and reserve a few tablespoonfuls of the juice.

Butter a 1.2 litre/2 pint pudding basin. Cut a round from one slice of bread to fit the bottom of the bowl, then cut the rest into sections to fit the sides, reserving some for the top. Dip one side of each slice in the reserved juice, then use it to line the bowl, soaked-side out. Gently spoon in the cooled fruit, arrange the lid pieces to fit tightly, then cover with baking parchment or foil. Put a small plate or saucer on top and weigh it down with a tin can so that the juice will seep into the bread. Keep any juice which spills over. Allow the pudding to cool, then refrigerate overnight.

To serve, run a knife around the edge between the bread and the bowl and turn out on to a deep plate. Pour any remaining juice over the top. Serve with custard or whipped cream, if you like.

Overleaf: Caragh Lake, County Kerry.

A GREEN FOOL

*The creamy, unctuous qualities of the avocado are not often
used in sweet dishes. Combined here with the last of the summer
gooseberries, the fruit brings a new twist to the classic fool.*

675 g/1½ lb gooseberries
1 large, ripe avocado
grated zest and juice of 1 lime
caster sugar
langues de chat (see below), biscuits or
    Macaroons (see page 154), to serve

Wash, top and tail the gooseberries and cook until soft and the
juice runs. This can be done in the oven or gently on the stove,
but the microwave is ideal because the berries seem to keep their
colour. Purée the gooseberries in a food processor and then sieve
to remove the seeds.

Peel, stone and chop the avocado and immediately toss it with
a little of the lime juice.

Return the gooseberry purée to the processor, add the avocado
and blend until creamy. Sweeten the purée to your taste with the
caster sugar, add the lime zest and the juice of half the lime.
Chill for at least an hour. Serve in glasses, with pretty biscuits
or Macaroons.

Note: to make *langues de chats*, or cats' tongues, to go with the
fool, cream together 75 g/3 oz butter and 75 g/3 oz caster
sugar until pale and creamy, then mix in 3 unbeaten egg whites.
Fold in 75 g/3 oz plain flour, then pipe 5 cm/2 inch strips of the
mixture on lined baking trays and bake in a preheated oven at
200°C/400°F/Gas Mark 6 for 6–8 minutes until golden brown
round the edges. Using a spatula, carefully transfer to a wire rack
to cool.

PEARS POACHED IN WHITE WINE

110 g/4 oz caster sugar
2 cinnamon sticks
grated zest of 1 small orange
a bottle of sweet white wine, e.g. Muscatel or similar
6 pears
1 tablespoon lemon juice
grated nutmeg, to decorate

Put the sugar, cinnamon sticks, orange zest and wine in a
saucepan which will just hold the pears upright. Heat the liquid
gently until the sugar is dissolved, and then boil hard for a few
minutes to create a light syrup.

Peel the pears carefully, leaving the stalks on and brushing with
lemon juice. Trim the bottoms slightly, so they will stand upright.
If there is insufficient liquid to come up to the stalks, add water.
Poach in the wine for about 15 minutes, or until they are tender
but not too soft. When the pears are cooked, remove and cool.

Take the cinnamon sticks out of the poaching liquid and boil the
liquid hard, uncovered, until it forms a thin syrup. Leave to cool.
Pour the syrup over the pears and grate a little nutmeg over the
top just before serving.

Right: Blarney Castle, Cork.

QUEEN OF PUDDINGS

SERVES 6

Here is a lighter version of this perennial favourite, which seems to please young and old alike.

5 eggs
450 ml/¾ pint whipping cream
300 ml/½ pint milk
a small piece of cinnamon stick
1 teaspoon grated lemon zest
½ teaspoon vanilla extract
2 tablespoons caster sugar, for the pudding
75 g/3 oz fresh breadcrumbs
4–5 tablespoons raspberry jam
175 g/6 oz caster sugar, for the meringue

Separate 3 of the eggs and set the whites aside for the meringue. Beat the remaining eggs and yolks together with the cream, milk, flavourings and 2 tablespoons sugar. Put the breadcrumbs in an ovenproof dish, pour the cream mixture over them and set aside for an hour or two to allow the crumbs to swell.

Preheat the oven to 160°C/325°F/Gas Mark 3.

Bake the pudding for 15–20 minutes until set. Allow to cool for a few minutes, then spread the jam over the surface. Raise the heat to 190°C/375°F/Gas Mark 5.

Beat the egg whites until they form stiff peaks. Sprinkle 75 g/ 3 oz sugar in slowly, whisking continuously, and then fold in the remaining sugar thoroughly.

Spread the meringue over the jam evenly and bake for 15 minutes until the meringue is just set and slightly brown, keeping an eye so it doesn't burn.

CHRISTMAS PUDDING

SERVES 6

While today's taste is for lighter food, an exception is always made in favour of the traditional Christmas pudding, although it, too, is evolving – butter is widely used today instead of suet and there hasn't been any meat in it for almost a hundred years.

175 g/6 oz glacé cherries

225 g/8 oz candied peel

75 g/3 oz each walnuts and blanched almonds

350 g/12 oz breadcrumbs

55 g/2 oz plain flour

225 g/8 oz light brown sugar

1 large apple, peeled and chopped

225 g/8 oz each raisins, currants and sultanas

1 tablespoon ground mixed spice

350 g/12 oz butter or shredded suet

8 eggs

a large glass of Irish whiskey or sherry

175 ml/6 fl oz Guinness

salt

Cut the cherries in half. Thinly slice the candied peel and then chop it finely. Coarsley chop the nuts. Mix all the fruit together with the breadcrumbs, flour, sugar, apple, dried fruit, spices and a pinch of salt. Add the suet, if using, otherwise soften the butter and gradually beat in the eggs, with the whiskey or sherry. Pour this mixture into the dry ingredients and mix well. Add enough of the Guinness to give a dropping texture, but don't make it too runny.

Place discs of baking parchment in the bottoms of two 850 ml/ 1½ pint pudding basins and butter them well. Fill the bowls two-thirds full, leaving room for expansion. Cover the tops with more buttered paper and then cover well with foil. The puddings will take 5–6 hours steaming. They can also be cooked at a low heat in the oven, standing the bowls in a tin of water and enclosing both tin and bowl completely in foil, making a sort of steam-proof tent, for 5–6 hours at 150°C/300°F/Gas Mark 2. When cooked, allow to cool before removing the foil.

Cover with fresh baking parchment and more foil before storing in a cool place until required. The puddings will require a further steaming of 1½–2 hours, before they are served.

Note: the puddings can be left overnight in the refrigerator before cooking, if it's not convenient to cook them immediately.

Opposite: Brandon Bay and the Cloghane sea inlet.

CINNAMON TOAST

A tea-time treat for children of all ages.

thick slices of white bread
butter
ground cinnamon
light brown sugar

Toast one side of the bread. Butter the untoasted side generously, sprinkle liberally with the cinnamon and then the sugar. Brown under the grill and eat immediately, while the buttery cinnamon runs down your chin.

A BOWL OF BISHOP

MAKES ABOUT 8 GLASSES

This was the favourite 'night-cap' of the eighteenth century, famed in song and verse. Jonathan Swift wrote about it, though when his friend Stella made it for him, the oranges were roasted in front of the fire, and the wine heated with a hot poker.

4 oranges
20 cloves
1 cinnamon stick
2–3 pieces of mace
1 teaspoon allspice berries
600 ml/1 pint water
a bottle of ruby port
sugar lumps or caster sugar
1 nutmeg
juice of 1 lemon

Preheat the oven to 180°C/350°F/Gas Mark 4.

Make incisions in 2 of the oranges, press the cloves into them and roast for half an hour or so until they make a slightly hissing sound.

Put the whole spices in the water in a saucepan (if you can't get whole or blade mace, use a nutmeg or more allspice berries) and boil until reduced by half. In another saucepan, heat the port gently, then ignite it to burn off some of the alcohol and concentrate the flavour. (If you can't bear to do this, then don't bother!)

Put the port, spice water and roasted oranges into a large bowl, ideally one which can be kept warm, and add sugar to taste. Slice the remaining oranges into the bowl, grate in some more nutmeg and sharpen the flavour with lemon juice.

BAKING

IRISH CURD TART

The ancient poetry of Gaelic Ireland has many images of feasting on rich curds, and these tarts are still enjoyed today.

450 g/1 lb cottage cheese
juice and grated zest of 1 lemon
2 tablespoons caster sugar, plus a little extra
55 g/2 oz ground almonds
4 eggs
2 tablespoons raisins
grated nutmeg

FOR THE PASTRY
75 g/3 oz butter
140 g/5 oz flour
1 tablespoon caster sugar
1 egg yolk, beaten
1–2 tablespoons very cold water

Make the pastry in the usual way, rubbing the butter into the flour and sugar and moistening with the egg yolk and 1–2 tablespoons of water, as required. Roll out to fit a greased 20 cm/8 inch tart tin and chill for 30 minutes.

Preheat the oven to 180°C/350°F/Gas Mark 4. Cover the pastry case with baking parchment or foil, fill with baking beans and bake for 10 minutes. Remove the paper and beans and bake for a further 5 minutes until just golden. Set aside while you make the filling.

Blend or sieve the cottage cheese, lemon zest, sugar and ground almonds. Sharpen to taste by adding a little lemon juice. Beat the eggs, then fold thoroughly, with the raisins, into the cheese mixture. Pour into the prepared pastry case and sprinkle a little sugar and grated nutmeg over the top. Bake for 30–40 minutes until golden brown. The mixture will gently subside as it cools.

Serve warm or cold. A little whipped cream is good with it, if it's to be served warm.

Note: the raisins can be soaked in a spoonful of whiskey for a few hours first, to plump them up and give a little extra flavour.

Previous page: Winter snows across Glencar, County Kerry.

SIMNEL CAKE

SERVES 10

The Simnel cake has been associated with Easter since medieval times and after the 40 days of Lenten fast it must have been a delicious, spicy treat. Ready-bought marzipan will speed up the preparation time.

110 g/4 oz butter
75 g/3 oz brown sugar
2 tablespoons golden syrup
4 large eggs
250 g/9 oz self-raising flour
1 teaspoon each ground cinnamon, grated nutmeg and ground ginger
350 g/12 oz mixed dried fruit
110 g/4 oz candied peel
1 tablespoon apricot jam, warmed

FOR THE MARZIPAN
450 g/1 lb ground almonds
225 g/8 oz caster sugar
225 g/8 oz icing sugar
2 eggs
2 teaspoons lemon juice
a few drops of almond extract

To make the marzipan, sift the almonds with the sugars. Beat the eggs, lemon juice and almond extract together and stir into the almond mixture, kneading well until a smooth paste is formed. Break off eleven walnut-sized pieces, roll into balls and set aside (these were said to represent the twelve apostles of Jesus, minus Judas). Divide the remaining piece of paste in two and roll into two rounds that will fit the cake tin.

To make the cake, preheat the oven to 160°C/325°F/Gas Mark 3 and grease and line a 20 cm/8 inch cake tin. Cream the butter, sugar and syrup together. Add the eggs, beating well after each addition. Sift the flour and spices together, then fold into the mixture thoroughly. Fold in the fruit and candied peel.

Place half the mixture in the prepared tin and gently cover with a layer of marzipan. Put the remainder of the mixture on top. Bake for one hour, then cover with a piece of foil and reduce the heat to 150°C/300°F/Gas Mark 2 and cook for a further half an hour. Test with a skewer, which should come out clean; remember not to push it down into the marzipan layer. When cooked, transfer to a wire rack and allow to cool for an hour or so. Remove from the tin and continue cooling.

When the cake is firm, after about half an hour, spread the apricot jam over the top of the cake, then press the second marzipan round on top, knocking up the edge decoratively. Put the cake under the grill, not too close to the heat, for a few moments to toast the top. Watch it carefully, as it burns quickly. Now dampen the marzipan balls and press them around the top of the cake. Lower the grill rack and return the cake to the grill, to toast the balls. Tie a wide yellow ribbon around the cake for a festive appearance.

CHOCOLATE CAKE WITH MOCHA FILLING

SERVES 8

This delicious chocolate cake is perfect for a luxurious afternoon tea or a dinner party dessert to celebrate St Valentine's Day.

FOR THE CAKE

225 g/8 oz plain flour

75 g/3 oz cocoa powder

4 large eggs, separated

5 tablespoons sunflower or rapeseed oil

225 g/8 oz golden granulated sugar

FOR THE FILLING

75 g/3 oz butter

110 g/4 oz icing sugar, sifted

2 teaspoons instant coffee, dissolved in 1 tablespoon hot water

1 tablespoon rum

TO DECORATE

450 ml/¾ pint double or whipping cream

1 tablespoon caster sugar

175 g/6 oz good dark chocolate

Preheat the oven to 190°C/375°F/Gas Mark 5 and grease and line a 20 cm/8 inch cake tin.

Sift the flour and cocoa together. Beat the egg yolks, oil and sugar together until pale and creamy. Fold in the flour and cocoa. Beat the egg whites to a soft, dropping consistency and fold carefully into the flour mixture. Pour into the prepared tin, making a depression in the centre. Bake for about 45 minutes. Test the cake with a skewer; if it comes out clean, the cake is cooked.

Cool the cake in the tin for 10 minutes before turning it on to a cake rack. When cold, split the cake in half horizontally.

To make the filling, beat the butter to a cream with the icing sugar, then beat in the coffee solution and rum. Spread lavishly on the bottom layer and sandwich the cakes together. Any surplus filling can go on the top of the cake.

Whip the cream with the caster sugar until soft. Reserving some for decoration, cover the entire cake. With a potato peeler, pare some large flakes of chocolate for the top of the cake, then grate the remainder. Cover the sides of the cake with the grated chocolate, using a palette knife. Pipe or spoon the reserved cream around the top and scatter the chocolate flakes in the centre.

HOT CROSS BUNS

MAKES 12–14

Hot cross buns are synonymous with Easter, though, in fact, they are now thought to predate Christianity. Whatever their origins, they are delicious, especially toasted with plenty of butter. They are incomparably better homemade and, with dried yeast, very easy to make.

675 g/1½ lb plain flour

15 g/½ oz sachet easy-blend dried yeast

2 teaspoons sugar

1 teaspoon salt

3 teaspoons ground mixed spice, or to taste

55 g/2 oz butter

300 ml/½ pint warm milk

1 large egg, beaten

140 g/5 oz mixed dried fruit

55 g/2 oz candied peel

110 g/4 oz sugar and 300 ml/½ pint water, boiled together to form a syrup

Mix the flour, dried yeast, sugar, salt and mixed spice together. Soften the butter in the warm milk and add the beaten egg. Make a well in the flour and pour in the liquid, drawing in the flour from the sides and kneading well until a pliable dough has formed (this can be done in a food processor or mixer). Knead in the fruit and peel. Cover the dough with clingfilm and allow to rise for an hour or so.

Knock the air out of the dough and knead again for a few moments. Divide into 12–14 pieces and shape into balls. Arrange these on oiled baking trays, cover and leave to rise for a further 20–30 minutes.

Mix 2 tablespoons of flour and 1 tablespoon of water together and trail a cross on the top of each bun. Preheat the oven to 190°C/375°F/Gas Mark 5. Bake for about 20 minutes (they will sound hollow when tapped underneath). With a pastry brush, paint the buns with the syrup and return to the oven for 5 minutes, to set.

WHOLEMEAL SCONES

MAKES 12 SCONES

Almost every Irish household has its own recipe for 'brown scones'.

½ teaspoon salt
3 teaspoons baking powder
175 g/6 oz plain white flour
400 g/14 oz coarse wholemeal flour
55 g/2 oz brown sugar
75 g/3 oz butter
2 eggs
240 ml/8 fl oz milk
butter, to serve

Above: Derrynane and Kenmare Bay, Ring of Kerry.

Preheat the oven to 220°C/425°F/Gas Mark 7.

Sift the salt and baking powder with the white flour and mix thoroughly with the wholemeal flour. Add the sugar and rub in the butter with your fingers. Beat the eggs and milk together. Reserve a tablespoon or so, and fold the rest quickly and very lightly into the flour, working as little as possible. If necessary, add a little more milk to form a relaxed dough.

Roll out on a floured surface to 2.5 cm/1 inch thick and cut into rounds or squares. Brush the tops with the reserved milk and egg.

Bake for about 20 minutes, or until there is a hollow sound when the scones are tapped underneath. Serve warm, split and buttered.

STRAWBERRY CHOCOLATE ROLL

SERVES 6

Swiss rolls and chocolate rolls are a favourite component of the tea table. This strawberry-filled chocolate roll is rich enough for an elegant summer dinner party.

FOR THE CAKE
75 g/3 oz plain flour
30 g/1 oz cocoa powder
½ teaspoon baking powder
2 large eggs
110 g/4 oz caster sugar
2 tablespoons hot water
icing sugar, sifted, to decorate

FOR THE FILLING
240 ml/8 fl oz double cream
55 g/2 oz caster sugar
brandy or vanilla extract, to taste
450 g/1 lb strawberries, cleaned and hulled

Preheat the oven to 220°C/425°F/Gas Mark 7.

Butter a 30 x 23 cm/12 x 9 inch Swiss-roll tin and line with baking parchment. Cut another piece of parchment the same size and have ready a tea-towel, to be wrung out in hot water.

Sift the flour, cocoa and baking powder. Beat the eggs and sugar together until thick, white and creamy. With a large metal spoon, fold in the flour, cutting with the edge of the spoon, and turning, rather than mixing. Finally, fold in the hot water. Pour into the tin, smooth with a palette knife and bake for 7–10 minutes until the mixture has slightly shrunk away from the sides. If the sponge is overcooked, it becomes dry.

Put the piece of baking parchment on the hot tea-towel and sprinkle it with sugar. Turn the cake out on top. Quickly trim the edges, then peel the baking paper away carefully. With the help of the hot tea towel, roll up the sponge from the long side, enclosing the paper inside. (The hot towel helps to prevent cracks forming in the sponge). Leave to cool.

Stiffly whip the cream with a little sugar and brandy or vanilla extract. Roughly chop three-quarters of the strawberries, then fold them into the cream. Carefully unroll the chocolate roll, remove the paper and fill with the strawberry mixture. Roll up the cake and filling, then dredge with a little icing sugar. Decorate with the remaining strawberries.

AUTUMN APPLE TART

FOR THE PASTRY

175 g/6 oz plain flour

30 g/1 oz caster sugar

110 g/4 oz butter

1 egg yolk

1 tablespoon lemon juice

salt

cream or crème fraîche, to serve

FOR THE FILLING

3 large Bramley cooking apples

3 large red dessert apples

1 tablespoon grated lemon zest

caster sugar, to taste

1 tablespoon lemon juice

1 tablespoon melted butter

2 tablespoons icing sugar

Armagh has been renowned for more than 200 years for the quality of her apples. This tart combines two types of apple – Bramley cooking apples for the purée; and eating apples, which hold their shape when cooked, for the decorative slices.

To make the pastry, sift the flour with a pinch of salt. Stir in the sugar. Rub the butter into the flour and salt with the fingertips, or pulse in the food processor. Beat the egg yolk with the lemon juice and mix in. Add a few drops more cold water if required. Roll out or pat into a greased 23 cm/9 inch tart tin. Chill while you prepare the filling.

Peel, core and roughly chop the cooking apples and cook gently until soft, adding a spoonful of water if necessary. Press through a sieve or purée and add the grated lemon zest. Sweeten to taste with caster sugar. When cold, spread over the bottom of the pastry.

Preheat the oven to 190°C/375°F/Gas Mark 5.

Quarter and core the unpeeled red apples, cut into neat slices and brush with lemon juice. Arrange the slices in a circle around the tin, on top of the purée, covering it completely. Brush the slices with melted butter and then use a sieve to sprinkle a little icing sugar over the top.

Cover the apple slices with a circle of foil and bake for about

APPLE DUMPLINGS

SERVES 6

'Coleridge holds that a man cannot have a pure mind who refuses apple dumplings. I am not certain but he is right.'
Charles Lamb, The Essays of Elia

6 large dessert apples
2 tablespoons lemon juice
5 sticks of rhubarb or 450 g/1 lb plums,
    stoned, or a mixture of both
2 tablespoons sultanas
55 g/2 oz butter
150 g/5 oz golden granulated sugar
6 cloves
675 g/1½ lb shortcrust or puff pastry,
    homemade or bought
1 egg, beaten
ice cream, to serve

Preheat the oven to 180°C/350°F/Gas Mark 4.

Peel the apples and brush with lemon juice. Remove the cores, then remove and reserve a little more apple from the centres to widen the cavities. Wash and chop the rhubarb or plums, add the reserved apple and the sultanas and cook gently in 30 g/1 oz butter until soft but not mushy (a few minutes in a microwave is ideal). Fill the cored apples with the fruit mixture, sweeten to taste, reserving a tablespoon of sugar for sprinkling, and add a clove to each. Top with a knob of butter.

Cut the pastry into 6 pieces and roll them out to fit the apples. Set each apple on a square of pastry and dampen the edges. Draw up the corners, cut away the surplus pastry and press the edges well together, moulding to fit the apples. Roll out the pastry trimmings to make leaves and use these to cover any imperfections. Make steam holes in the top of the pastry, brush with the beaten egg and then sprinkle with the reserved sugar.

Bake for about 45 minutes until the pastry is golden brown. Very large apples may take a little longer. A skewer pressed into the side will tell if it is done. Vanilla ice cream is very good indeed with apple dumplings.

Note: cooking apples can be used for the apple dumplings if you like very tart flavours, but add extra sugar.

MARBLE CAKE

SERVES 8–10

Marble cake has fascinated children for generations and it is always a popular feature of the tea table.

200 g/7 oz plain flour
1 teaspoon baking powder
salt
75 g/3 oz good dark chocolate or 1 tablespoon cocoa powder
    mixed with 2 tablespoons milk
175 g/6 oz butter
175 g/6 oz caster sugar
3 large eggs
grated zest and juice of a small orange

Below: Killorglin and River Laune, Ring of Kerry.

Preheat the oven to 180°C/350°F/Gas Mark 3.

Sift the flour with the baking powder and a pinch of salt. Melt the chocolate, if using, over hot water. Beat the butter in a large bowl until soft, then add the sugar and continue beating until the mixture is pale and creamy. Add the eggs, one by one, adding a spoonful of flour with each and beating well after each egg. Fold in the remaining flour carefully in a couple of batches, making sure no pockets of flour remain. Transfer half the mixture to another bowl and add the orange zest and 1–2 tablespoons juice. Mix the chocolate or cocoa mixture gently but thoroughly into the first bowl.

Drop the mixtures into a buttered and lined 900 g/2 lb loaf tin, 3 spoonfuls of one and then the other until you have used all the mixtures. Finally, draw a knife through the mixture diagonally from each end of the tin to create a marbled effect.

Bake for 45 minutes, or until the cake has shrunk slightly from the sides of the tin. Cover with foil if the top is browning too quickly. Leave to cool briefly in the tin, then transfer to a wire rack.

LONGFORD CAKES

MAKES 6 LARGE OR 12 SMALL TARTS

My mother made little apple and almond tarts as an alternative to mince pies at Christmas. Many years ago I came across a recipe for Longford Cakes, which had a similar filling, in a book published in 1935. The author was a Lady Sysonby, who may have had connections with Lord and Lady Longford through literary and theatrical circles in Dublin and London, so perhaps that is how the name arose.

These delicious mouthfuls are simple to make for afternoon tea. Made larger, in 10 cm/4 inch tart tins, they make a good dessert with a little ice-cream or the geranium-scented cream on the side.

FOR THE PASTRY

280 g/10 oz plain flour, sifted
1 tablespoon caster sugar
175 g/6 oz butter
2 egg yolks
1–2 tablespoons cold water
salt

FOR THE FILLING

2 tablespoons ground almonds
5 tablespoons apricot jam
100 g/3½ oz walnuts, chopped
5 tablespoons sultanas
2 tablespoons very finely chopped apple
1 tablespoon grated lemon zest
1 egg, beaten, to glaze
caster sugar, to decorate

FOR THE GERANIUM CREAM

240 ml/8 fl oz double or whipping cream
2–3 scented geranium leaves, washed and dried

To make the pastry, mix together the flour, sugar and a pinch of salt. Rub in the butter, and then moisten with the egg yolks, adding a tablespoon or so of cold water as required. Chill for 30 minutes.

Preheat the oven to 190°C/375°F/Gas Mark 5. For the larger version, grease and line six 10 cm/4 inch tartlet tins; for smaller cakes, use well-buttered patty tins. Roll out the pastry very thinly and line the tins, gathering the trimmings and re-rolling to make the lids.

Mix all the filling ingredients together, chopping any large pieces of apricot in the jam, and divide among the tarts. Dampen the pastry edges and put on the lids, press well together to seal and tidy up the edges. Glaze with beaten egg, make vents in the tops and sprinkle with sugar. Bake for 25–30 minutes until the pastry is golden brown.

To make the geranium cream, softly whip the cream, then infuse the leaves in the cream for several hours. Serve with the cakes.

ORANGE CARAWAY CAKE

SERVES 10

Caraway seeds, immensely popular in Irish cooking since at least the seventeenth century, are as popular today. This variation on the seed or Madeira cake is very good. Without the orange and marmalade, this makes an excellent plain seed cake, always on hand to offer with a glass of sherry or Madeira when friends call.

110 g/4 oz butter
110 g/4 oz light brown sugar
225 g/8 oz plain flour
1¼ teaspoons baking powder
2 large eggs
2 tablespoons fine cut marmalade
1 tablespoon caraway seeds
grated zest and juice of 1 orange
2 tablespoons icing sugar, sifted
salt

Preheat the oven to 160°C/325°F/Gas Mark 3.

Cream the butter and sugar until light and fluffy and pale in colour. Sift the flour with the baking powder and a pinch of salt. Add the eggs, beating them in one at a time, adding a tablespoon of the flour with each. Add the marmalade, the caraway seeds and the orange zest and juice, then fold in the remaining flour. Pour into a well greased 23 cm/9 inch ring mould.

Bake for about 45 minutes. Cool slightly before turning out. When cold, dredge the cake with icing sugar.

MACAROONS

These classic macaroons are a favourite element of the 'biscuit tin', often offered with a glass of sherry or a cup of tea.

rice paper
2 large egg whites
110 g/4 oz ground almonds
almond or ratafia extract
225 g/8 oz caster sugar
30 g/1 oz rice flour
flaked almonds

Preheat the oven to 160°C/350°F/Gas Mark 4 and line two baking trays with rice paper or baking parchment.

Lightly whisk the egg whites with a fork. Mix the ground almonds, extract, sugar and rice flour together. Mix in the whites thoroughly. Using a teaspoon, drop spoonfuls of the mixture on to the rice paper, well apart, and top each one with an almond flake.

Bake until just golden brown, about 10–12 minutes. Remove, still on the rice paper, to a rack to cool. When cold, tear or cut away the excess rice paper from the edges of the biscuits. The rice paper is, of course, edible.

WALNUT CAKE

SERVES 10

280 g/10 oz plain flour
100 g/3½ oz walnuts
200 g/7 oz butter, at room temperature
175 g/6 oz caster sugar
4 large eggs, at room temperature
1 teaspoon vanilla extract
grated zest and juice of 1 lemon

Preheat the oven to 180°C/350°F/Gas Mark 4 and butter and line a 900 g/2 lb loaf tin.

Sift the flour. Crumble the walnuts with your fingers. In a large bowl or mixer, cream the butter, then add the sugar, beating until pale and creamy. Add the eggs, one by one, adding a tablespoon of flour and beating well between each. Mix in the walnuts, vanilla and 1 tablespoon lemon juice. Mix them in well, then fold in the remaining flour, in 3 parts, cutting it in rather than beating it, but making sure no flour pockets remain. Transfer the mixture to the prepared tin and sprinkle the top with lemon zest. Place a piece of foil loosely over the top.

Bake for about an hour, lowering the heat to 160°C/325°F/Gas Mark 3 and removing the foil after half an hour. Test with a skewer after 45 minutes. When cooked, cool for a few minutes in the tin before removing to a wire rack.

The cake can be iced with a little icing sugar, mixed with a tablespoon of lemon juice and spread over the top. It will keep for a few days in a tin.

Note: the walnuts can be toasted for 5 minutes in the oven for a nuttier flavour, but watch carefully because they burn quickly.

BARM BRACK

'Barm' is the yeasty ferment produced when brewing ale or beer; 'brack', or breac, refers to its speckled nature. Barm brack is one of the few Irish traditional breads or cakes raised with yeast, and, like hot cross buns, the origins are lost in antiquity. It is an essential part of the Hallowe'en festivities and, like colcannon, usually contains a ring – whoever gets the ring will be married within the year.

4–5 saffron strands
2 tablespoons water
560 g/1¼ lb plain white flour
1 teaspoon salt
55 g/2 oz brown sugar
2 teaspoons ground mixed spice, or to taste
15 g/½ oz sachet easy-blend dried yeast
75 g/3 oz butter
350 g/12 oz mixed dried fruit and candied peel
2 eggs, beaten
300 ml/½ pint warm milk

TO GLAZE
1 tablespoon sugar
4 tablespoons water

Put the saffron to soak in the water for 15 minutes.

In a large bowl, mix the flour, salt, sugar, spice and dried yeast together. Rub in the butter and then add the fruit and candied peel. Add the beaten eggs and the saffron mixture to the warm milk. Make a well in the flour mixture and pour in the liquid, reserving a tablespoon. Mix well together, drawing in the flour from the sides. When the mixture will hold together, turn out and knead for 5–6 minutes. Return to the bowl and cover with clingfilm. Allow to rise for about 1½ hours in a warm place.

Grease two 20 cm/8 inch cake tins and, if you are adding rings, wrap them in greaseproof paper. Turn the dough out and knead again briefly, then divide between the cake tins. Press the rings into the centre and allow to rise for a further 30 minutes.

Preheat the oven to 220°C/425°F/Gas Mark 7. Brush the cakes with the reserved liquid and bake for about 10 minutes, then reduce the heat to 190°C/375°F/Gas Mark 5 and bake until a hollow sound results when the bottom is tapped, about 40–50 minutes. Make a glaze with the tablespoon of sugar and the water, boiled together until reduced to a syrup. Brush over the bracks and return to the oven to set for 5 minutes.

Note: rings can be bought in baking supply shops.

SODA BREAD WITH ONION

SERVES 6–8

This variation on classic Irish soda bread is especially good with potted meats and pâtés.

1 large onion, finely chopped
4 tablespoons olive oil
500 g/1 lb 2 oz strong white flour
½ teaspoon salt
1 teaspoon bicarbonate of soda
600 ml/1 pint buttermilk
2 teaspoons caraway seeds

Preheat the oven to 180°C/350°F/Gas Mark 4.

Chop the onion finely and cook in a heavy pan, in a tablespoon of the oil until dark brown and crisp but not burned. Cool.

Sift the flour and salt together. Dissolve the bicarbonate of soda in 1 tablespoon buttermilk. Add this, with the remaining 3 tablespoons olive oil, to the buttermilk. Add the onions and seeds to the flour. Make a well in the centre and add the liquid. With a fork, mix it all together thoroughly, mixing lightly until you have a fairly smooth texture, but don't knead.

With floured hands, shape the mixture into a round cake, cut a cross in the top, transfer to a greased baking sheet and bake until the loaf gives a hollow sound when tapped on the bottom, about 40 minutes.

Note: if buttermilk is not available, use fresh milk and 2 teaspoons of baking powder instead of the bicarbonate of soda.

PRESERVES

LOGANBERRY AND PLUM JAM

MAKES 5 X 225 G/8 OZ JARS

It seems more like fun to make small quantities of different jams with whatever is to hand, and this intensely flavoured combination is well worth the half-hour it takes. If there are no gooseberries, use more lemon juice.

450 g/1 lb plums
110 g/4 oz gooseberries
450 g/1 lb loganberries
900 g/2 lb caster sugar
juice of ½ lemon
425 ml/15 fl oz water

Simmer the plums and gooseberries in the water until the plums are soft enough to remove the stones. Cut the plums in pieces, if they are large, and return them to the water. Add the loganberries, bring back to the boil and cook for 5 minutes. Remove from the heat, pour in the sugar and lemon juice and stir until completely dissolved.

Boil hard for 7–10 minutes until a few drops cooled on a chilled saucer will wrinkle when pushed with the finger. Pour into hot, sterilised pots and cover. The jars can be sterilised in the oven or dishwasher.

RASPBERRY JAM

MAKES 5 X 250 G/12 OZ JARS

The raspberry season is so short, but jams and preserves help to prolong the taste of summer.

1.4 kg/3 lb caster sugar
1.4 kg/3 lb raspberries
225 g/8 oz redcurrants
2 tablespoons lemon juice

Put the caster sugar into an ovenproof dish and warm gently in the oven.

Put the fruit in a stainless steel saucepan over a very low heat until the juice begins to flow, then bring very slowly to the boil and simmer for 10 minutes. Pour in the warmed sugar and lemon juice, and stir until the sugar has completely dissolved.

Boil hard until it sets when tested. Start testing after 8 minutes. Put some saucers to chill in the freezer and then test by putting a few drops of the mixture on a saucer and allowing to cool. If the surface of the drop wrinkles when pushed with a finger, the jam is ready. Pot in hot, dry, sterilised jars and seal immediately.

Previous page: Slea Head and Coumeenoole Beach.

ROSE-PETAL VINEGAR

Use this delicate vinegar to flavour summer salads, or try a few drops on summer fruits, such as strawberries and raspberries; it seems to bring out the flavours. The choice of the base vinegar is important. Use a good-quality white-wine vinegar, or organic cider vinegar. Rice vinegar, which can be bought from oriental shops, is particularly delicate in flavour.

Measure equal quantities of vinegar and scented rose petals, about 2 large cupfuls of each. Put them together in a glass container and cover tightly. They should be left to steep on a sunny window for at least 3 weeks. If you like a stronger flavour, strain off the petals and add fresh ones, then steep a little longer. Strain into bottles and cork tightly. Elderflower vinegar can be made the same way.

Below: Glandore Village, County Cork.

CHRISTMAS CHUTNEY

MAKES ABOUT 5 X 350 G/12 OZ JARS

900 g/2 lb Bramley or other cooking apples
350 g/12 oz onions, finely chopped
300 ml/½ pint white-wine or malt vinegar
225 g/8 oz white sugar
75 g/3 oz brown sugar
225 g/8 oz mixed nuts, e.g. chestnuts, walnuts and almonds
2 teaspoons ground ginger
grated zest and juice of 1 lemon
1 teaspoon salt

Peel, core and chop the apples. Cook the onions in the vinegar until soft. Add the apples, cook for 3–4 minutes, and then add the remaining ingredients and simmer gently until the mixture begins to thicken, lowering the heat and stirring frequently to prevent it from burning.

Pot into warm, sterilised jars with plastic-lined lids (metal would react with the vinegar).

Note: chutneys improve with keeping, the flavours becoming more subtle after about 2–3 months. If the chutney is made for immediate use, wine vinegar is best as malt vinegar needs time to mellow.

ROWANBERRY JELLY

MAKES 6 X 350 G/12 OZ JARS

The rowan tree, or mountain ash, like the elder tree, had important magical properties for our Celtic ancestors. The red berries make an excellent jelly for game, hams and pâtés, the flavour maturing as it ages. Rowanberry jelly can be used instead of redcurrant jelly in sauces and with lamb.

1.4 kg/3 lb rowanberries
2 large Bramleys or other cooking apples,
    coarsely chopped
grated zest and juice of 1 lemon
granulated sugar

Put the rowanberries in a large saucepan and crush them slightly. Add the coarsely chopped apples (no need to peel or core) and lemon zest. Just cover with water and cook until both are very soft.

Strain overnight, through a jelly bag. An old linen tea-towel over a large plastic colander can be used. Be careful not to squeeze the bag – it must drip naturally, or the jelly will be cloudy.

Measure the juice collected, add the lemon juice, and allow 450 g/1 lb sugar to 600 ml/1 pint liquid. Boil hard until a few drops on a chilled saucer will wrinkle when pressed with a finger. Pot into hot, sterilised jars with plastic-lined lids and seal tightly.

Overleaf: Sea inlet mountains, Dingle Peninsula, County Kerry.

Acknowledgements

I would like to thank Christine Cullen for her generous assistance in preparing the manuscript and her helpful suggestions throughout the work. I'd also like to thank Eveleen Coyle and Fleur Robertson for the idea and for their confidence and patience, and my cooking friends and colleagues for inspiration.

This edition published in the United Kingdom in 2015 by
Pavilion
1 Gower Street
London
WC1E 6HD

ISBN 978-1-90910-894-3

A CIP catalogue record for this book is available from the British Library.

10 9 8 7 6 5 4 3 2 1

Reproduction by Colour Depth Ltd, UK
Printed and bound by 1010 Printing International Ltd, China

This book can be ordered direct from the publisher at www.pavilionbooks.com

Editor: Fleur Robertson
Editor of new edition: Emily Preece-Morrison
Home economy: Valerie Berry
Styling: Davina Perkins
Recipe photography: Tony Briscoe
Landscape Photography: Michael Diggin Photography